Pillars of Paul's Gospel

Galatians and Romans

by

John F. O'Grady

PAULIST PRESS
New York, N.Y./Mahwah, N.J.

Cover mosaic of St. Paul courtesy of Scala/Art Resource, NY.

Library of Congress Cataloging-in-Publication Data

O'Grady, John G.
    Pillars of Paul's gospel: Galatians and Romans/by John F. O'Grady.
        p.   cm.
    Includes bibliographical references and index.
    ISBN 0-8091-3327-X (pbk.)
    1. Bible. N.T. Galatians—Criticism, interpretation, etc.
    2. Bible. N.T. Romans—Criticism, interpretation, etc. 3. Paul,
    the Apostle, Saint. I. Title.
    BS2685.3.037   1992.
    227'.106—dc20   91-45556
                                                             CIP

Published by Paulist Press
997 Macarthur Boulevard
Mahwah, New Jersey 07430

Printed and bound in the
United States of America

CONTENTS

Section IV
Pauline Theology

Conclusion

There is neither Jew nor Greek, there is neither slave nor free, there is neither male nor female, for you are all one in Christ Jesus.

—Galatians 3:28

For the women in my life who continue to teach me that we are all one in the one God.

For my sisters:
>Ave O'Grady Hobson
>Eleanor Virginia O'Grady, R.S.M.

In Albany:
>Winifred Firsching Buehler
>Mary Lou Howes Brennan
>Diane Payst Connolly

In Pittsburgh:
>Constance Leahy Taylor

In Chicago:
>Agnes Cunningham, S.S.C.M.

In Miami:
>Arlene Segal Friedman
>Mary Ann Jungbauer
>Loretta Elizabeth Mulry, I.H.M.
>Judith Shield, O.P.

PREFACE

Paul's personality has long intrigued me. His writings have often confused me and his history has amazed me. His personality is only glimpsed in his writings but we can develop a portrait of a driven person, subject to outbursts of enthusiasm, instilled with a passion for what he preached and often frustrated with both his converts and other apostles. He even struggled with persecution and possibly failure. His writings often confuse precisely because of the depth of his thought and of his approach to the gospel. His history amazes since he never knew the historical Jesus and went from being a persecutor to being the apostle to the Gentiles.

All three aspects are interrelated: personality, writings and history. No one can attempt to understand one without studying the others. That of course can cause further problems since we do not have a full picture of his personality, do not possess all of his writings, and even his history is limited and further confused by the material found in the Acts of the Apostles.

This work is not intended to be a definitive study of Paul nor of the two letters under consideration, Galatians and Romans. It attempts to interrelate personality, writings and history based upon current levels of research. I am indebted to several contemporary Pauline scholars whose works will be cited either in the text or in the bibliography. Further study can be made of these individual authors.

The text is intended for anyone interested in a beginning study of Paul and in particular these two great epistles which for me are in truth: *Pillars of Paul's Gospel*. College students studying one course on Paul should find this book helpful as should any adult involved in a scriptural course on Paul. I have written with both audiences in mind.

The reader will also be expected to read the letters along with the

1

text. I would suggest that the reader first read the passage under discussion from the New Testament and then, after reading the text, return again to the passage discussed. This should help in gaining better insights into what Paul intends. Throughout the work I will frequently quote from the New Testament and in general I will be using the Revised Standard Version. Occasionally I will use my own translation. Readers may choose any edition of the New Testament for study.

The first four chapters should be studied quickly to allow the students to get into the actual text of Paul as soon as possible. Depending upon time limitations, the final three chapters on Pauline theology may be assigned for additional reading by the student. I would strongly urge, however, that a careful presentation and discussion on justification always be included.

As with all that I have written, I am indebted to both fellow New Testament exegetes and to the support of friends and staff here at Barry University. Paul Achtemeier in his writings and addresses has always managed to capture my interest because of his ability to discover neuralgic points in the New Testament. Both he and the Rev. Raymond E. Brown, S.S. through their research have assisted me greatly in attempting to reconstruct some of the historical factors surrounding Paul's history and the history of the Roman Christian community. Drs. Laura Armesto, and Mary Ann Jungbauer have read the manuscript and offered some much needed advice. To all, I offer my gratitude.

The sunshine of South Florida continues to remind me of the goodness of God which clearly shines as well in the life and writings of the person we call the apostle to the Gentiles. I hope that this study will encourage others to devote the time and energy merited by the letters of Paul to the Galatians and to the Romans.

Miami
Feast of Saints Peter and Paul
June 29, 1991

SECTION I

Paul and His Environment

Chapter 1

THE APOSTLE PAUL AND HIS BACKGROUND

"I advanced in Judaism beyond any of my own age among my people, so extremely zealous was I for the traditions of my fathers" (Gal 1:14). "[I was] circumcised on the eighth day, of the people of Israel, of the tribe of Benjamin, a Hebrew born of the Hebrews, as to the law a Pharisee" (Phil 3:5). But this same, Paul in Greek circles, Saul in Jewish circles, experienced the risen Lord Jesus and history was changed. The Hebrew, the Pharisee, the Roman, became a Christian and helped chart the course for the religion that circled the globe, formed western culture, transformed lives and continues to exert its power for good in the lives of more than a billion people.

Jesus came and taught and died and rose and left for his followers to continue his preaching. No one had a greater influence in the early transmission of the Jesus tradition to the Gentiles than Paul of Tarsus. With him the teaching of Jesus reached out beyond the confines of Judaism. He made applications, drew conclusions, formed communities, provided leadership, corrected, cajoled, loved and admonished. Paul traveled and suffered and prayed and preached and called and built and died.

Almost two thousand years later the thought of Paul and his interpretation of the Jesus tradition continue to challenge Christians. His insights into the meaning of Jesus still disturb and call to conversion. Years from now followers of the Lord Jesus will read and reread the writings of Paul, forever mining of the wealth deposited by this great early preacher and apostle.

Of the 657 pages of Greek text of the New Testament almost one-fourth comes from Paul. In addition almost one-half of the con-

Authentic Pauline Letters Accepted by All		
Romans	1 and 2 Corinthians	Galatians
Philippians	1 Thessalonians	Philemon
Letters Rejected as Pauline		
1 and 2 Timothy	Titus	Ephesians
Hebrews		
Letters Whose Authorship Is Disputed		
Colossians	2 Thessalonians	

tent of the Acts of the Apostles deals with Paul. Yet this Hebrew, Pharisee, Roman citizen was not a follower of Jesus, not an eyewitness, not someone who experienced Jesus in his ministry. His stamp on Christianity cuts deeply. His influence on contemporary Christianity, in particular Roman Catholic Christianity, however, seems less powerful. Often Christians, especially leaders of the church, have trouble understanding Paul and implementing his thought within the church. Some of the problems come from the New Testament itself which seems to present different Pauls. The Paul of Acts does not always seem to be the same person found in the letters. With regard to the letters themselves, much depends on what letters are accepted as authentically Pauline. Even in those genuine Pauline letters, development seems to have taken place in his thinking, so that Paul in Galatians differs from Paul in Romans even when dealing with similar topics. Further development is found in Philippians, especially in christology.

No one should claim that understanding Paul is easy. His background, his mind, his experiences interact and ebb and flow together. No wonder that many Christians do not like Paul or just leave Paul alone. Some think he is a chauvinist and claim that the second-class status of women in the church can be traced to him. How happy many American women were when they decided to take their hats off in church and the male-dominated church went along. All this in spite of Paul's comment in 1 Corinthians that "the head of a woman is her husband . . . but any woman who prays or prophesies with her head unveiled dishonors her head . . . a woman ought to have a veil . . ." (1 Cor 11:3–16).

Yet, unless the followers of Jesus pay careful attention to the writings of Paul and seek to understand his interpretation of the Jesus tradition, that Christian faith lives an impoverished life. Paul enriches and rewards the effort to delve into the labyrinth of what often seems confusing and too complicated to matter.

Paul's teaching on grace and freedom and justification expresses an important aspect of the Jesus tradition that constantly needs to be reaffirmed. Paul is not everyone's favorite apostle. He never will be such. None of his letters have become favorite books of the New Testament in the same way that people love the gospel of Luke, or who are enthralled by the gospel of John. Yet, what Paul teaches, Christianity desperately needs.

Paul was a Jew educated as a Jew but living in a Greek environment, influenced by Jewish religion as well as by popular and refined culture. Paul was intelligent and committed and given to flights of fancy expressed in enthralling poetry in some of his letters. Paul lived on the edge, never shrinking from a challenge. He made friends and enemies and claimed independence and humbly accepted the outreach from those who loved him. Given to extremes, Paul would likely have made a first class scoundrel had he not decided to accept his experience of the risen Lord and become the apostle to the Gentiles.

Jewish Background

Paul boasted of his life as a Jew of the Pharisaic traditions. He was more Jewish than most and proud of it.

Paul the Jew

I advanced in Judaism beyond many of my own age among my people, so extremely zealous was I for the traditions of my fathers (Gal 1:14–15).

Circumcised on the eighth day, of the people of Israel, of the tribe of Benjamin, a Hebrew born of Hebrews, as to the law a Pharisee, as to zeal a persecutor of the church, as to righteousness under the law blameless (Phil 3:5–6).

Are they Hebrews? So am I. Are they Israelites? So am I. Are they descendants of Abraham? So am I (2 Cor 11:22).

Throughout his writings he seems to think in Old Testament categories and frequently uses images from the Jewish scriptures. Paul believed that the one God spoke to humankind through the Jewish scriptural traditions, and continues to speak to humankind in the Jesus tradition. Almost all of the teaching of Paul about God and humankind finds its foundation in his Jewish background. Frequently he explicitly quotes from the Old Testament and seems to use the Greek translation (the Septuagint, henceforth referred to as the LXX). Following the practice of other rabbis, Paul accommodates an Old Testament text, or gives a new interpretation, allegorizes it, changes its context, creating a unity between the Jewish traditions and the newer Jesus tradition.

Although Paul grew up in Tarsus, a Roman city, and formed part of the Jewish diaspora (those living outside of Palestine) the nearness of Tarsus to Jerusalem would have afforded opportunities for Paul to visit the city on the great feasts. The synagogue in Tarsus would have been the gathering place to read the scriptures in their Greek translation (LXX), and even the feeling of nationalism enkindled by the Maccabean revolt would have contributed to the enthusiasm of Jews in the diaspora for their national origins.

In Acts 22:3 Luke states that Paul studied Judaism under Gamaliel, the son of Hillel, a rabbi at the time of Christ who was rather moderate with regard to the law of Moses. A sympathetic or conciliatory attitude characterized Gamaliel as witnessed in Acts: "If this plan or this undertaking is of men, it will fail; but if it is of God, you will not be able to overthrow them. You might even be found opposing God" (Acts 5:38–39).

Whether Paul studied under Gamaliel or not, whether he once planned to become a rabbi or not, we experience a good deal of rabbinical exegesis in his letters. Citing Isaiah 49:8: "At the acceptable time I have listened to you and helped you on the day of salvation," Paul refers to Jesus and his followers: "Now is the acceptable time; behold, now is the day of salvation" (2 Cor 6:2). In Romans 5 Paul develops the image of Adam as a type of the one who is to come. Jesus becomes the second Adam. Paul demonstrates his rabbinic training in his use of the Old Testament as he preaches to Jews of the meaning of the gospel of Jesus.

Perhaps Paul grew tired of the moderation and conciliatory attitude associated with Gamaliel, for he tells us that he was on the road to Damascus to persecute Christians and bring them back to Jerusalem in chains. Paul, dissatisfied with the slowness associated with moderation, attempts to do something about it in his own way. Fortunately, at this time he experienced the risen Lord.

To travel to Damascus, with the hope of bringing back captives, Paul must have had some authority. In all probability he had the support of the sanhedrin in Jerusalem. They would have chosen delegates to represent them who were learned in the law and possessed some degree of eloquence. We know from his letters that Paul had both. Paul the Jew traveled to Damascus and became Paul the Christian.

In his letters Paul makes specific reference to his pre-Christian life as a Pharisee (Phil 3:4–5). He also speaks of his zeal for the traditions of his fathers (Gal 1:14). He clearly used the technical rabbinic vocabulary for receiving and transmitting traditions (1 Cor 15:3), argues in the rabbinic manner, and even relies on certain rabbinic traditions (1 Cor 10:1–5). Finally, the apostle's efforts to relate the Jesus tradition to the law of Moses manifests a continuing influence on Paul by the Pharisaic traditions. His letters show that Paul was truly a Pharisee and continued to use his traditions in the service of the gospel.

Also from Judaism, Paul inherited an appreciation of apocalyptic ideas. Vast libraries exist on the meaning of the apocalyptic. Simply: apocalyptic literature encourages people to remain faithful, for things will get worse before they get better. And now we have no indication when things will get better. Paul may reinterpret some of these ideas, but he writes of the wrath of God (Rom 1:18), the judgment to come for all (1 Cor 4:5), the suddenness of the end (1 Thes 5:1–4) and the power that God exercises in setting the time (Gal 4:4). Taken out of context these apocalyptic ideas would give the impression that Paul emphasized doom. He seems to have been influenced by Jewish apocalyptic writings but such teachings fall under the more powerful influence of his understanding of gospel. From Judaism he accepted some of these traditions but used them to suit his own preaching of the Jesus tradition. The apocalyptic would give way to the eschatological which saw the future of humankind in God and that alone would offer hope and encouragement.

Throughout this work I will make frequent references to the Old Testament and Paul's Jewish background. Only if readers understand whence Paul came can they hope to appreciate his interpretation of the Jesus tradition. But Paul was not only influenced by Judaism, Paul also drank from the well of the popular culture in a Roman city.

Paul the Cosmopolitan Greek

Paul used a Roman name. (We can find no foundation that he changed his name from Saul to Paul after his conversion. Probably he had two names: one used in Jewish circles and the other in Greek or

---

APOCALYPTIC LITERATURE

The Book of Daniel: the Jews are suffering persecution under the Seleucid king Antiochus IV.

Mark 13: Christians in Rome are suffering persecution by Jews and Romans.

The Book of Revelation (Apocalypse): Christians are suffering persecution principally by the Roman authorities.

Roman circles.) He quoted the Old Testament in Greek (LXX). He wrote his letters in Greek and they show a good Greek education. Often his mode of expression and composition show some influence from classical Greek rhetoric. The Greek style of argumentation called diatribe can also be found in his letters as Paul debates with an imaginary interlocutor.

Paul's images are frequently Hellenistic and derived from a city culture. Political, commercial and legal terminology coming from a Greek culture appear in his letters. In his ethical teaching he used common Greek vocabulary for "freedom," "conscience," "nature," "moral excellence," "self-sufficiency." Living in Tarsus with a Greek education Paul experienced the culture which was the heir of ancient Greece. His journeys also contributed to a development in Paul of Hellenistic culture but at Tarsus we can find sufficient foundations for Paul's eclectic background.

Situated on the river Cydnus, Tarsus lies a few miles north of the Mediterranean just below a pass through the Tarsus mountains in southeast Asia Minor (Turkey). The location of the city as a crossroads in the ancient world made Tarsus a lively center of commerce and trade. Romans, Greeks, traders from the east shared a common life at the stadium for games, at the baths, in the forum and marketplace. The theater also flourished with plays dealing with pride, guilt, vengeance, human passion and grief. As a city of learning Tarsus ranked with Alexandria and Athens. From this city came Athenodorus the Stoic who was tutor to Octavian Augustus. The city experienced as well the fading of the old gods of Mount Olympus and the introduction of the mystery religions of the east with their magic and astrology and exotic cultic practices.

No one could live in such a city and not feel its influence. The

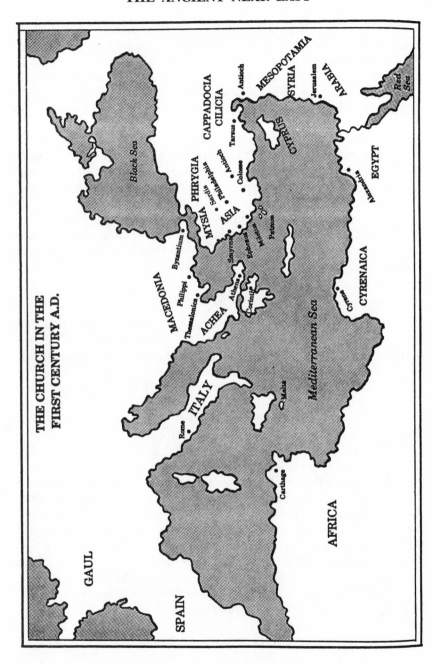

THE CHURCH IN THE
FIRST CENTURY A.D.

eastern religions enchanted people with their ritual washing, their sacred meals and the promise of life through union with a particular god or goddess. Incipient gnosticism with its myth of a descending redeemer offering the true knowledge of salvation must have fascinated the intellectual and religious circles of the city. Who would not feel some pull from this environment! Neither Paul nor Christianity, however, derived some of its practices from these eastern religions or gnosticism. Rather, as people universally felt the need for union with the divine through ritual, so Paul and Christianity offered a response to that need. The new religion was not imposed from without but met an inner need as people wrestled with the meaning of life in a polyglot culture. Paul may have recognized that certain ideas or practices from his environment would find fulfillment in his understanding of the Jesus tradition. All came from a common anthropological need and the similarity lies in humanity rather than in a borrowing from each other.

Paul the Roman

Finally Paul was a Roman. In an empire of more than a hundred million people, only about five million were Roman citizens. For Paul to claim such heritage implies that his family came from a rather high station in life. He makes no reference to them, and so we can presume they were not Christians. All we know, remarkable in itself, is that a Jew had acquired Roman citizenship.

The Roman empire encompassed a universal hope for unity. From the Persian Gulf westward to the outposts of Britain the empire prevailed. Paul envisioned a universal religion in a unified world. The *Pax Romana* with its language, its system of communication and commerce, afforded the new religion ample opportunities for growth and development. The road system alone assisted the great apostle to the Gentiles to make his missionary journeys. Paul began his letter to the Romans acknowledging "I am under obligation both to Greeks and barbarians, both to the wise and foolish" (Rom 1:14). Born in a city forming a crossroads of the empire, the citizen of Rome developed a feeling for unity and universality. He saw Jesus of Nazareth as the one who could give peace and deliverance from sorrow as Caesar had given peace and deliverance from the sword.

Paul the Complex Believer

In every human life multiple facets express the complexity of the unifying person. The more we know about someone: background,

THE ROMAN EMPIRE

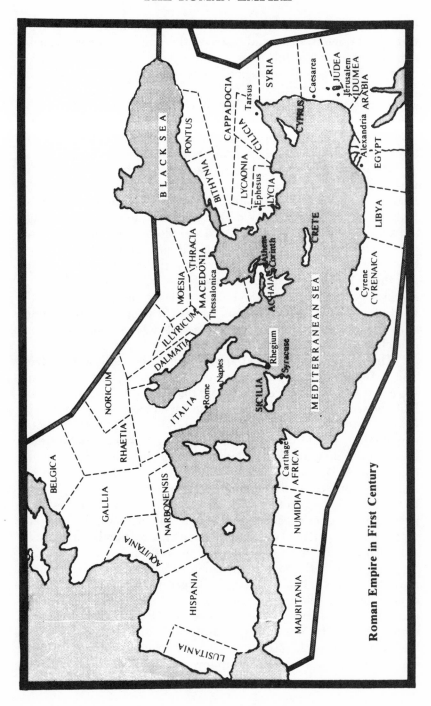

Roman Empire in First Century

family, interests, education, experiences, the more we can see through the multiplicity and discover the unity. Paul was probably more complex or multiple than most. We have some of his letters. We have a somewhat "whitewashed" view of him by Luke in Acts. We have other letters attributed to him by later followers or even by some who just claimed his authority. His temperament was far from gentle. He boasted of his independence from the other apostles, confronted Peter, called people foolish, set rules and regulations—and the Jesus tradition was never again the same.

If we can understand some of the historical background of Paul we can understand more of him and his writings. The mixture of Pharisaic Judaism and its devotion to the law and apocalyptic Judaism with its call for fidelity in the midst of pain and suffering intermingle in Paul the Christian. Greek culture and philosophy, the cosmopolitan effects of a great Roman city, allowed some of the unity of Paul to be expressed in great multiplicity. Move through that multiplicity, and the unity that is Paul of Tarsus, Hebrew, Pharisee and Roman, sparkles. Not everyone will love Paul or his writings, but perhaps the level of appreciation should rise. At least if people have "trouble" with Paul now, they can all take some satisfaction that the ancient church equally had "trouble" with Paul.

The thought of this great apostle cannot be easily categorized. The existing sources comprised only occasional letters and not learned treatises. Paul preached more than he wrote, and in all probability he wrote more letters than those which have come down to us. Certain principal themes weave in and out of his letters, but often enough these great themes of Christianity such as grace and justification and freedom are folded into anxieties and concerns about his communities. His temperament did not allow him the leisure to rest and reflect and carefully compose his thoughts. Rather, Paul seems like the harried executive who dashes off a letter while between planes, running hither and yon, trying to balance too many projects with too many personal demands from too many friends and enemies alike. No wonder people have trouble with Paul!

This book will deal in particular with Galatians and Romans, those two pillars of Pauline thought. Before examining these letters in detail, however, the reader needs a fuller appreciation of their author. We know he was a Jew, educated as a Greek as well, living in a cosmopolitan city, intelligent, headstrong, independent, tireless in his efforts to preach to the Gentiles, often intolerant of opposing views, and, in all, a committed follower of Jesus of Nazareth. It all

CONVERSION ca. C.E. 36

1 Thessalonians C.E. 49–50 from Corinth
1 Corinthians C.E. 53–54 from Ephesus
Galatians C.E. 54 from Ephesus
2 Corinthians C.E. 55 from Macedonia
Philemon C.E. 56–57 from Ephesus
Romans C.E. 57–58 from Corinth or Cenchreae
Philippians C.E. 57–58 from Ephesus

began with his conversion, his religious experience on the road to Damascus.

STUDY QUESTIONS

1. What aspects of Paul's personality are appealing? Which are not? Do any bother you?

2. Is Paul's Jewish background important in understanding his approach to the Jesus tradition? How is this expressed in his understanding of Jesus?

3. Paul had many influences in his life and thought. How could one compare his experience to the contemporary world and how would this influence religious traditions?

4. Is the presence of apocalyptic themes in Christianity important? Do they make any sense today?

5. Why would faith in Christ help to unify the complex personality of Paul?

6. Are there aspects of Paul's personality that could help the contemporary believer?

Chapter 2

PAUL'S RELIGIOUS EXPERIENCE

The core of every religion is religious experience. Religion rests upon the human response to the world as we experience it but only if that experience of the world includes the presence of the divine or the transcendent. A true religious experience also includes an awareness of a personal God and not just an appreciation of some force or power. All the great religions of the world rest upon the religious experience of one person or of a group of people. Whether we deal with Moses and the Jewish people on Sinai, Jesus and his baptism, the early followers of Jesus and his resurrection, Mohammed and his hajira, or Joseph Smith and his revelation by an angel, all deal with a religious moment in history which gave birth to a religious movement.

Throughout human history individuals have been unsettled about questions of life and destiny, creation and God, and the fitting response to these felt realities. Earlier peoples recognized the presence of gods or goddesses in nature and sought appropriate responses to acknowledge this presence. They rendered worship, the natural outcome of the religious experience. The combination of sensing the presence of the transcendent as personal and then becoming aware of this presence in human life naturally brings about some knowledge of the divine. Love follows this knowledge, and people express their devotion in worship. Certain chosen people fulfill a destiny for others in being able to recognize this presence. They offer both understanding and love to those who will listen. Finally, they encourage the response of worship to the transcendent one experienced in some unusual way. The level of understanding becomes the preaching which eventually becomes recorded in writing for future generations. The knowledge gained from the preachers lay the foundation for the

RELIGIOUS EXPERIENCES AND RELIGION

Abraham in Ur	Judaism
Moses in Horeb	Judaism
Jesus in the Jordan	Christianity
Apostles at Easter	Christianity
Paul on the Road to Damascus	Christianity
Muhammed near Mecca	Islam
Martin Luther in Wittenberg	Lutheranism
Joseph Smith in Palmyra	Mormons

way of life associated with the experience, and particular acts of ritual and worship follow. Usually much is asked of these chosen people, and they respond obediently to the presence of their God. Often their lives are not easy. They suffer as they try to express the meaning of the religious experience to others. They also feel the pain of rejection and misunderstanding as people refuse to acknowledge the God who has entered into their lives and called them to speak the word which gives light.

Abraham had his experience of God and gave up his past to follow this God. He traveled from Ur of the Chaldees to Haran and then to Canaan following this call (Gen 11:31–12:6). Later this same God would ask Abraham to give up his future in the offering of his son Isaac. Abraham experienced the presence of a personal God and in obedience responded in worship. His acceptance of the call of God brought suffering as well as blessings.

Uneasiness about life → openness to religious experience

Religious experience → preaching to others

Preaching to others → common worship

Common worship and preaching → recording preaching in writing (sacred books)

Sacred books → guidance for future generations

Moses traveled to Horeb and had his experience of God in the burning bush (Ex 3:1–3). He knew that the transcendent was present, and the God who revealed himself to Moses did so personally as he proclaimed to Moses, "I will be what I will be" (Ex 3:14), implying that this God would be present in the history of Moses and of his people. Moses had further experiences of God, particularly at Sinai, and here he was surrounded by the Jewish people (Ex 19), who became the people of this personal God and offered worship. Both Moses and the Jewish people experienced the pain that comes from acknowledging the presence of the living God as well as the blessings flowing from a life dependent upon this same God.

Throughout the history of the Old Testament, various prophets experienced God and felt the divine imperative to preach the word of God. Isaiah, Jeremiah, Ezekiel and a host of other men and women recognized the divine in the personal God of their fathers and, willingly or not, became spokespersons for this God in teaching the people and offering worship. They fulfilled their ministry to others, but not without great personal cost. Blessings and sufferings seem to characterize all who hear the call of God and respond.

Jesus himself had his religious experience, dramatically described by Mark 1:9–11, Matthew 3:13–17 and Luke 3:21–22, in his baptism. Traveling to Jerusalem, Jesus hears John the Baptizer, goes into the Jordan to be baptized by John, and a voice declares Jesus as Son. Jesus responds by preaching the coming of the kingdom of God. The call to live as God's holy Son ultimately brought Jesus into a ministry that would lead to the cross before he experienced the resurrection. Jesus also experienced blessings and suffering.

All of these religious figures share a common humanity which forms the foundation for the religious experience which in turn creates the possibility for religion. We cannot possibly understand any religion without appreciating this anthropological basis. People need to respond to their religious dimension and depend on chosen men and women to help them in understanding and living a life founded on the presence of God.

Contemporary theologians consider Friedrich Schleiermacher (1768–1834) as the theologian of religious experience. Living in a period when religion had become relegated to an unimportant aspect of human life compared to the cultural and aesthetic, Schleiermacher sought to show that human life needs religious experience. Religion also needed its empirical basis found in the common daily affairs, rather than in the obscure or extraordinary. "The self-identical essence of piety is this: the consciousness of being absolutely depen-

MYSTERIUM TREMENDUM	→ Fear, anguish, pain, run away, avoid, dread, the unknown, the terrible, the frightening, unworthy
MYSTERIUM FASCINANS	→ Awe, curiosity, seduction, delightful, promising, enticing, wanting to be near

dent or, what is the same thing, of being in relation with God" (Schleiermacher, 15). All the great religious people of all religious traditions, but especially the Judaeo-Christian tradition, accepted this sense of dependence upon a personal God.

Rudolf Otto also grounded religion in human experience. Otto criticized Schleiermacher's analysis of dependence which does not sufficiently safeguard the qualitative difference between the experience of God and other human experiences. For Otto, "creature consciousness" characterizes the true experience of God (Otto, 24). The experience of God as *mysterium tremendum* evokes a double response: awe and fascination and fear and terror. In the presence of the divine we are filled with dread, *mysterium tremendum*, and drawn by wonder, *mysterium fascinans* (Otto, 2).

A careful analysis of the religious experience of Moses or Isaiah, for example, shows the combination of fear and fascination. Inextricably they are drawn into the closeness of the divine while at the same time experiencing fear and dread. They are unfit to enjoy such an experience. The religious experience of Jesus in his baptism seems to have the sense of the *mysterium fascinans*, but the sense of unworthiness or dread is expressed by John.

William James was a pragmatist interested in the effect of religious or mystical experiences on people. In his study he records several examples of mystical or religious experience, all of which help to understand all religious experiences.

Historically, all of the great religious moments in the lives of religious leaders demonstrate these qualities. Moses and Isaiah are passive in the presence of God; they experience God only in a transient way; they have insights to offer to others and often they have

RELIGIOUS EXPERIENCE IN WILLIAM JAMES

1. *Ineffability:* only those who have had the experience can understand it; it cannot be "named."
2. *Noetic:* the experience not only concerns emotion, but yields insights.
3. *Transiency:* the experience not only lasts for a short time but it is not subject of complete accurate recollection or recall.
4. *Passivity:* although the state can be induced and many require careful preparation beforehand, the experience itself involves a sense of passivity (James, lectures, 16, 17).

trouble in explaining to others what has happened to them. Most of these elements can also be found in the analysis of the story of Abraham or of the baptism of Jesus. Whatever happened to these great religious leaders, the traditions have shown certain common elements: each has a religious personality; in almost every case they are on a journey, whether a figurative journey as they travel toward God or an actual journey when they experience God. Journeys and light seem to be some of the common elements in religious experiences even of some of the great philosophers. Rousseau was traveling to see Diderot when he had his illuminating experience. Descartes dreams he is traveling and speaks of fire. Pascal is not traveling but sees a light.

Paul on the Road to Damascus

The religious experience of Paul on the road to Damascus exemplifies all of these elements. Paul has his sense of dependence, experiences awe and fear, cannot sufficiently describe the experience, and gains insights. The moment is transient and Paul meekly accepts the nearness of his Lord and obeys. The divine imperative to preach which Isaiah, Jeremiah and Ezekiel experienced became the mandate for Paul to proclaim the good news of Jesus to all the nations.

The Acts of the Apostles contains three different accounts of the experience: Acts 9:1–19; 22:1–21; 26:1–32. Paul himself refers to this experience in Galatians 1:11–24 and 2 Corinthians 4:4–6. Luke's first account is a narrative which explains Paul's ministry as an apostle. In the second account Paul appears before the Jews in Jerusalem, and in the final account he appears before the Roman governor. Paul's

ACCOUNTS OF PAUL'S EXPERIENCE

Acts 9	*Acts 22*	*Acts 26*
Light from heaven	Light from	Midday light
voice saying to him	heaven about noon	brighter than
		sun
Companions heard	Voice saying to	All experience
voice	him	light
Companions saw	Companions saw	Voice saying
nothing	light	to Paul
Paul rises, blinded	Companions	Companions
	heard nothing	hear nothing
Enters Damascus	Enters Damascus	
stays three days		
Ananias comes	Ananias comes	

accounts in Galatians and Corinthians should be preferred in trying to understand the exact meaning for Paul himself. Luke offers his analysis of the experience, but the actual testimony is colored by his particular theology and Luke's need to offer testimony to future generations. Better to rely on the testimony of Paul himself as the primary source for understanding what happened and precisely what it meant to Paul.

PAUL'S RELIGIOUS EXPERIENCE IN GALATIANS

Persecuted the church
Tried to destroy it
God revealed Jesus to Paul
Began to preach to Gentiles
Went to Arabia
Returned to Damascus
Gal 1:11–17

Paul the Roman citizen, resident of Tarsus, master of Jewish law, educated in the culture and philosophy of Hellenism, travels to Damascus with letters empowering him to arrest Christians. On the way a bright light blinds him. No single event apart from the resurrection of Jesus himself has determined the course of human history.

The first account of the religious experience of Paul recorded by Luke seems to emphasize that Paul can be ranked with the other apostles because he has experienced the risen Lord. In the second account by Luke the emphasis on the light and the mention of glory remind the reader of the death of Stephen, so perhaps in this account Luke wishes to emphasize the role of Paul as martyr or witness. Finally, in the third account in Acts, Paul becomes the prophet calling for conversion and reform, a message common to all the prophets (Stanley, 315–338). In each instance, Luke depends upon his own theology and adapts the circumstances to suit his established purpose. This analysis does not imply that Luke had no historical circumstances describing the religious experience of Paul but rather that he put these circumstances within his own perspective.

For all of the differences, certain elements remain constant: the time is around midday, Paul falls to the ground (note there is no mention of any horse), and he hears a voice and experiences a bright light. A comparison of the accounts seems to show that Luke uses his literary freedom to emphasize the light. In the second and third accounts, he mentions midday. In the second account, Luke describes the light as dazzling, and in the final account the light is brighter than the sunshine.

Throughout the Old Testament, the glory of God is associated with light. In Exodus, Moses stood in the cleft of the rock and shielded himself while the glory of God passed by (Ex 33:18–23). Isaiah also experienced the glory of God in the temple (Is 6). In the presence of the divine, the appropriate gesture is reverence demonstrated by falling to the ground. For Luke, Paul experienced the glory of God in Christ Jesus described in an "ineffable" way as a light brighter than the sun at midday. Luke has Paul question "Who are you?" with the answer, "I am Jesus," Paul becomes the evangelist, and, like Isaiah after his experience in the temple, Paul is willing to do whatever the Lord requests: "What will you have me do?" In Philippians, Paul will write that Jesus "apprehended" him and "lay hold of" him (Phil 3:12). Paul experienced the divine imperative and eventually became the apostle to the Gentiles.

Paul's contemporaries thought that his conversion was inexplicable: "And all who heard him were amazed and said, 'Is not this the man who made havoc in Jerusalem of those who called upon his name?' " (Acts 9:21). Something marvelous happened on the road to Damascus which changed Paul from a persecutor to an apostle.

In Galatians 1:11–24 Paul offers few details of his experience. He merely notes that he had been a persecutor and that God had chosen him from his birth (cf. Jeremiah 1:5) and revealed his Son to him. In 1 Corinthians 15:9, he acknowledged that he had persecuted the church and experienced the grace of God. In 2 Corinthians 4:4–6, he alludes to the glory of God. All we can really conclude from the actual letters of Paul about his conversion is that he considered himself the least of the apostles, and that he was blessed by God with a revelation of Christ and changed from a persecutor to an apostle. The moment was ineffable (Paul cannot adequately describe it), transient (it lasted for a moment in his life and had a profound effect), and noetic (Paul learned much, for he claims that his experience revealed the gospel to him). Throughout, Paul was passive (he submitted to the power of God, for God had chosen him from his birth).

Throughout the history of Christianity, many have attempted to explain exactly what happened. Could there be a natural explanation? Did Paul actually "see" the risen Lord? Was the experience, like a mystical experience, totally internal? Did Paul experience a sense of guilt because he had persecuted Christians (1 Cor 15:9) and sought release from this guilt by becoming a champion of Christians? The very nature of the experience precludes any ability to categorize the event. Something happened to Paul just as something happened to Abraham, Moses or Jesus. The reality of the experience gave birth to the preaching of the apostle to the Gentiles. That is sufficient. Many may attempt to analyze the event further than is recorded in the New Testament, but their conclusions will always be tentative. Better just to accept the reality of a religious experience which changed Paul from persecutor to preacher.

The journey is an interesting element. Throughout the history of religion, people have experienced the presence of the divine while undergoing a journey. Moses was journeying away from Egypt when he experienced the God of his fathers. Jesus was traveling from Nazareth when he experienced God his Father in his baptism by John. Martin Luther was traveling when he had his religious experience. Now Paul travels and experiences the glory of the risen Lord in a dazzling light. His "way" of living changes. Paul still journeys in life, but now the direction and destination are known and set. He follows the crucified savior and becomes the apostle who preaches the gospel of Jesus to the Gentiles.

We will never know exactly what happened to Paul for the very reason that the experience itself is inexplicable. Various images may be used to describe the event, but such a moment cannot be conceptualized and then translated into ordinary human words. No doubt Paul became aware of his creatureliness and dependence upon God. He also seems to experience a sense of awe that he, though unworthy, should be given such a marvelous moment in life. The noetic content is evident. Paul becomes an apostle, proclaiming and teaching and guiding based upon his experience. He did not need to be taught by the others, for his religious experience gave him the necessary knowledge to become the preacher. The moment itself was transient, lost in his past as he traveled for some thirty years preaching the good news about Jesus and obeying humbly the divine imperative, for he could do nothing else.

On the road to Damascus Paul becomes a Christian apostle. Paul who had lived as a dedicated Pharisee, critical of Christians and persecuting them for their beliefs, now acknowledges Jesus as the messiah. The crucified savior becomes the point around which the life of Paul now turns. This Jesus offers redemption from evil, sin and death. Paul proclaims this gospel with an enthusiasm that rivals any enthusiast of any century in any place.

The personality of Paul almost called out for such an experience. Whatever he did, he did wholeheartedly. All of his energies became funneled into this new way and this new preaching. The great persecutor became the great herald. He traversed the known world as an apostle to the nations. He wrote numerous letters, founded communities, offered guidance, established rules and guidelines, sent out other preachers, and formed systems of organization. God placed him on a certain path and Paul responded with all the energies of mind, body and soul. All we know and need to know is that Paul of Tarsus experienced the presence of the divine, the transcendent one, on the road to Damascus. That momentary experience of the glory of God by one person changed and continues to change the lives of hundreds of millions of people.

Paul's personality fascinates. He lived life with power and zest. He gave himself to life and to God and to Jesus of Nazareth. Did he dominate early Christianity as his writings dominate the New Testament? Did he fail to dominate early Christianity as his writings fail to dominate the Christian church today? Just what did he accomplish? And was he the great conqueror, moving from victory to victory, or was he, rather, a voice crying in the wilderness who failed more frequently than triumphed? Just who is the real Paul, and what does he offer to the Christian faith today? His greatest letter, the epistle to the Romans, gives us his legacy. We can understand this letter better if we also study the epistle to the Galatians. But before that we need further study of his historical situation vis-à-vis that of the other apostles and of the Jerusalem church.

STUDY QUESTIONS

1. Does everyone sometime in life have a religious experience?

2. A comparison between Paul, Abraham, Jesus and others seems to show an anthropological basis for religious experiences. How does this fit in with the idea of a revealed religion?

3. What do you like or dislike about the ideas of Otto and James? Are they helpful in understanding Paul?

4. Does it make any difference that we do not know exactly what happened on the road to Damascus?

5. All are on a journey. All need to experience God. How does this happen today and what does it mean for daily life?

6. Do religious personalities exist? Why? What does it mean to have a religious personality and how may this be expressed?

Chapter 3

PAUL AND JERUSALEM

Christians customarily think of Paul the great apostle to the Gentiles as moving from triumph to triumph. He had his religious experience and then began his missionary activities by preaching the gospel of salvation for all through faith. In fact, Paul may not have been as successful as we have thought. Perhaps Paul was less triumphant than triumphed over, and in the end he might even have seen his efforts to present his understanding of the gospel of Jesus as a failure. History makers often live and die as failures. Only later do many significant figures take on the role that life often denied them while alive. This should not surprise anyone. History recognizes millions of apparent failures who in death become the successes that eluded them in life. If Paul follows Jesus, then for even greater reasons we should not expect him to be a great success. Just as Jesus might be considered a failure in his ministry, the same might well be true for Paul. As Jesus triumphed in his resurrection, too Paul would triumph only in death.

When we compare Galatians to Romans, it seems that Paul changed his mind with regard to the question of the relationship between Christianity and Jewish law. Galatians carries with it an element of annoyance or even anger with regard to those who are not following the gospel that Paul preached. Paul tones down his approach in Romans. He seems willing to compromise and not demand full acquiescence to his understanding of the Jesus tradition. Perhaps Paul's approach to the Gentiles in Galatians and his original interpretation of the Jesus event was eventually transformed in favor of the approach of Peter, James and even Paul's fellow missionary, Barnabas. The dispute which took place at Antioch meant that the interpretation of faith coming from James and Jerusalem, which was other than that of Paul, would become normative. Paul and his understand-

Jerusalem Church	Paul	John
Circumcised and uncircumcised	Neither Jew nor Greek	All welcome
Law and works	Freedom and faith	Faith, love and freedom
Christianity continuation of Judaism	Radically new	Radically new
Limited understanding of Spirit	Emphasis on Spirit	Spirit is all

ing of the gospel would remain in his writings but would not become the dominant understanding of the Jesus tradition. No one will ever understand Paul without understanding what happened in his dealings with Peter, James and the Jewish/Christian community in Jerusalem and in Antioch.

Jerusalem and Antioch

In the beginning, Christianity struggled with the split between those who saw the teachings of Jesus as a continuation of the Jewish tradition with a system of doctrine and a code of ethics and those who saw the teachings of Jesus as a proclamation of the redemptive act of God in Jesus by which God opened the way, through faith, to reconciliation. Surely any believer today will say that it can and should be both. One position, however, can predominate, and for Paul salvation through faith was the basis of this new "good news." Historically, Paul's position failed to become the cornerstone of Christianity. Instead, historical Christianity opted for a way of living flowing more from the interpretation provided by the Jerusalem church.

Peter, James and the Jerusalem community advocated a continuation of the Jewish system, and this approach ultimately became the prevailing position in the earliest centuries. Paul, and possibly the Johannine community, held on to the emphasis of salvation as God's great gift through faith. This position needs constant study so that the good news of the gospel will always remain good news. Only a combination of both approaches can do justice to the teachings of Jesus. We need to return to the origins of Christianity and carefully attempt to reconstruct both the historical context and the theological conclusions of early Christianity coming from Judaism and its ultimate triumph in the Gentile world.

The reader of the Acts of the Apostles and the letter to the Galatians needs to reexamine this whole question of Jewish/Christian relationships as well as that of Jewish/Christian and Gentile/Christian relationships. The image that we often have of early Christianity struggling with the interpretation of the law and the ultimate victory of the compromise in Acts 15 needs more study. Usually we think that the dispute was resolved with freedom for the Gentile/Christian from Jewish observance, especially circumcision. But it may be that the question has deeper roots and that the teaching of Paul, the complete freedom, never became the dominant position. Far from writing to the Romans that he would go on to Spain as a triumphant apostle, perhaps it was his fervent hope that if he could go to Spain he would be able to preach his gospel there, free from the harassment of the followers of Peter, James and Barnabas.

Most people consider the event described in Acts 15:1–29, the council of Jerusalem and its decree, as the same event referred to by Paul in Galatians 2:1–10. Such need not be the case. First we should begin by claiming that any scenario describing Paul and his history should be taken from the letters of Paul and not from the Acts of the Apostles. As we have already noted, Luke has his own perspective dictating his use of historical events. In the past, most people presumed that in writing Acts, Luke presented an accurate history of the events narrated, therefore what was learned about Paul and his activities from the letters of Paul was set within the framework established by Luke. Today, we take Paul himself as the primary source and recognize that Luke may not have had full or accurate historical details, and that even when he had such information, he made adjustments to fit his purpose.

Acts 15:1–29

But some men came down from Judea and were teaching the brethren, unless you are circumcised according to the custom of Moses, you cannot be saved. And when Paul and Barnabas had no small dissension and debate with them, Paul and Barnabas and some of the others were appointed to go to Jerusalem to the apostles and elders about this question. . . .

When they came to Jerusalem they were welcomed by the church and the apostles and the elders, and they declared all that God had done with them. But some believers who belonged to the party of the Pharisees rose up and said: "It is necessary to circumcise them and to charge them to keep the law of Moses."

The apostles and the elders were gathered together to consider this matter. And after there had been much debate, Peter rose and said to them: "Brethren you know that in the early days God made choice among you that by my mouth the Gentiles should hear the word of the gospel and believe. And God who knows the heart bore witness to them giving them the Holy Spirit just as he did to us; and he made no distinction between us and them but cleansed their hearts by faith. Now therefore why do you make trial of God by putting a yoke upon the neck of the disciples which neither our fathers nor we have been able to bear? . . ."

James replied: "Brethren, listen to me. Symeon has related how God first visited the Gentiles to take out of them a people for his name. . . . Therefore my judgment is that we should not trouble those of the Gentiles who turn to God but should write to them to abstain from the pollution of idols and from unchastity and from what is strangled and from blood. . . ."

Then it seemed good to the apostles and elders with the whole church to choose men from among them and send them to Antioch with Paul and Barnabas. They sent Judas called Barnabas and Silas, leading men among the brethren, with the following letter . . .

"For it has seemed good to the Holy Spirit and to us to lay upon you no greater burden than these necessary things: that you abstain from what has been sacrificed to idols and from blood and from what is strangled and from unchastity. . . ." So they were sent off, they went down to Antioch, and having gathered the congregation together they delivered the letter. And when they read it they rejoiced at the exhortation.

Galatians 1:18–2:13

Then after three years I went up to Jerusalem to visit Cephas and remained with him fifteen days. But I saw none of the other apostles except James the Lord's brother. Then I went into the regions of Syria and Cilicia. . . . Then after fourteen years I went up to Jerusalem with Barnabas taking Titus along with me. I went up by revelation and I laid before them (but privately before those who were of repute) the gospel which I preach among the Gentiles, lest somehow I should be running or run in vain. But even Titus who was with me was not compelled to be circumcised though he was a Greek. But because of false brethren secretly brought in, who slipped in to spy out our freedom which we have in Christ Jesus, that they might bring us into bondage to them, we did not yield submission even for a moment that the truth of the gospel might be preserved for you. And from those who were reputed to be something (what they were makes no difference to me; God shows no partiality)—those I say who were of repute added nothing to me; but on the contrary, when they saw that I had been entrusted with the gospel to the uncircumcised, just as Peter had been entrusted with the gospel to the circumcised . . . and when they had perceived the grace that was given to me, James and Cephas and John, who were reputed to be pillars, gave to me the right hand of fellowship, that we should go to the Gentiles and they to the circumcised; only they would have us remember the poor which very thing I was eager to do.

But when Cephas came to Antioch I opposed him to his face because he stood condemned. For before certain men came from James he ate with the Gentiles; but when they came he drew back and separated himself fearing the circumcision party. And with them the rest of the Jews acted insincerely so that even Barnabas was carried away by their insincerity.

Galatians speaks of two visits by Paul to Jerusalem while Acts speaks of three. Galatians also refers to further contacts with the Jerusalem community but only through representatives who had been sent to Antioch.

After his conversion, Paul went to Jerusalem and conferred with Peter, remained with him for two weeks and also met with James (Gal 1:18). Paul visited Jerusalem a second time (Gal 2:1–10) fourteen years later and conferred with the "three pillar apostles." By this time, Paul would have established churches among the Gentiles, and his meeting in Jerusalem concerned specifically his mission to the Gentiles and the gospel that he preached to them. The outcome of this conference with the leading role played by Peter was an assurance that what Paul preached to the Gentiles in truth exemplified a proper understanding of the one gospel of Jesus and an assertion that he, in turn, was "to remember the poor." Paul willingly accepted this request, and in this meeting no expectations of circumcision, ritual or dietary or ethical demands were to be made upon the Gentiles in accepting Christianity. Paul was satisfied with the outcome of the meeting and evidently left to continue his missionary activity.

Sometime later Peter left Jerusalem, and perhaps at that time James assumed the head of the Jewish/Christian community there. For some unknown reason, the matter of observance of the law again became an issue, and, with Peter and Paul absent, the Jerusalem community formulated what has come to be called the apostolic decree as found in Acts 15. Gentiles were not obliged to observe circumcision but were to abstain from things sacrificed to idols, from blood, from what is strangled and from unchastity (Acts 15:29 and 21:25). If Gentiles did not observe these regulations, then no table fellowship could be possible with Jewish Christians. Peter heard of the decision and evidently withdrew from table fellowship. Paul confronted Peter as recorded in Galatians 2:11–13 and accused him and Barnabas of insincerity. This dispute at Antioch seems unresolved, since Barnabas and Paul separate and Paul, still holding on to his agreement to provide for the poor, plans a visit to Jerusalem, anticipating difficulties both from the Jews and from the Jewish Christians. In Romans he appeals to this community which had close ties with the Jerusalem church, to pray that he might "be delivered from the unbelievers in Judea, and that my service for Jerusalem might be acceptable to the saints" (Rom 15:30–31). The apostolic decree formulated without Paul was not accepted by Paul, for it veered away from the gospel of grace, salvation through faith. Evidently Paul left Antioch without any resolution of the requirements of Jewish observance for Gentiles, which in turn affected his understanding of the true meaning of the gospel.

Paul's Teaching and the Church

Many will no doubt not find this explanation too appealing. Protestants will not like the idea that the great apostle of the reformation was in fact not so successful in actual history and that his teaching ultimately gave way to the religious tradition that advocated a system of doctrine and an ethical code. Roman Catholics will not like it because it once again raises the whole problem of the reformation, with a renewed call to the legitimate gospel of Paul as salvation through faith alone with freedom for all believers. Roman Catholics may also have to rethink their own traditional view of the role of Peter in the development of Christianity and perhaps their interpretation of that famous quotation in Matthew 16:18–19 which appears around the interior dome of St. Peter's in Rome in which Peter is given the keys to the kingdom of heaven. This may in fact be a polemic against the apostolic authority that Paul himself claimed in Galatians 2:12–13. Much has yet to be studied with regard to the origin of early Christianity and of the development of the hierarchical church with its doctrine and ethics. We need not return to what Paul presented as an authentic interpretation of the Jesus tradition. All that is necessary is that more attention be given by all Christians to the teaching of Galatians and Romans.

Maybe if Christianity never had a close unity in the past, even at its origins, it never will have such a unity in human history and will have to live forever with the two approaches: the doctrinal system and ethical code and the salvation through faith alone. This is not a division between Roman Catholics and Protestants, since many Roman Catholics ascribe to the faith alone approach and many Protestants are more comfortable with the doctrinal system and ethical code, or at least a strong ethical code. All, however, Roman Catholic and Protestant, will recognize that the great support for the doctrinal system is the presence of the pope and church teaching authority which is the domain of Roman Catholics. Within this system the writings of Paul, especially Galatians and Romans, should play an important role.

Paul the Failure?

Paul was a failure in the tradition of Israel and Jeremiah and even Jesus, and for that reason he was a history maker. Peter may have triumphed along with James and Barnabas and others, but in fact it is the writings and teachings of the apostle to the Gentiles that continue to give guidance to Christianity and continue to disturb Roman Catholic Christianity. We have little, if anything, that can be ascribed to Peter or James. We have all of the writings of Paul in the New Testament, and we have Luke who tries to smooth things over and to offer us a history that presents compromise rather than a continual split.

During the initial period of the Gentile mission no effort was made to coordinate that mission with the type of Christianity associated with Jerusalem. That understanding of the Christian faith saw itself as an outgrowth of Judaism with its observance of the law. Soon, however, the law-free gospel of the Gentile church came into conflict with the legal framework of Jewish Christianity. The dispute came to a head at Antioch which is the conflict portrayed in Galatians 2:11–13. An earlier view held that the council of Jerusalem was convened and it was determined that Gentile Christians were free from circumcision but were obliged to observe those laws required by Leviticus to non-Hebrews living in the midst of Hebrews. Harmony was restored and Paul was free to continue his missionary activity in good conscience free from any harassment by those who wanted to require all Christians to become Jews. All of this is reported in Acts 15:1–2. Paul continued his successful activity as a missionary and, but for his arrest in Jerusalem, he would have continued his preaching in the west. It may be that Acts errs chronologically, but at least it was correct in portraying the successful resolution of the conflict between Paul and the leaders of the Jerusalem church. The final conclusion is that the unity was maintained in this early period of church history. This, we will see, became Paul's principal interest for which he was willing to compromise.

If, however, we pay attention primarily to the writings of Paul and not Luke, the apostolic decree of Acts 15 is understood not as the result of the conflict in Antioch as recorded in Galatians 2:11–14 but as the cause. If we follow the hint given in Luke that the dispute between Paul and Barnabas that resulted in their separation (Acts 15:36–40) was subsequent to the Jerusalem conference, then we can take seriously the opinion that the dispute at Antioch was the result of this conference. Thus there is no future conference to which we can appeal to restore the unity that was fractured in Antioch. Paul will seek that unity and promote that unity in his letter to the Romans but only after he has expressed his opinion in Galatians.

Antioch

Up to this time Paul felt secure that he was preaching a gospel with the support of the Jerusalem church and with the support of the Antioch community. After the dispute, he lost his power base in An-

---

PAUL AND JERUSALEM

Conversion C.E. 36.

Goes to Arabia.

C.E. 39 Paul goes first to Jerusalem and meets with Peter and also James.

C.E. 52 Thirteen years later, Paul goes to Jerusalem to meet with James, Peter and John (Gal 2:6b–10): the result was that Gentiles have freedom, and Paul should remember the poor.

C.E. 53 The apostolic decree is formulated (Acts 15). Paul was not present. Paul disputes with Peter, Barnabas and the men from James at Antioch when he hears of the new demands beyond his agreement to remember the poor. Paul's position is not accepted and Peter and Barnabas and others withdraw from table fellowship from those Christians who do not observe the Jewish law. Paul leaves Antioch and goes to Galatia.

C.E. 54 Paul writes Galatians

                                    Achtemeier, *The Quest* . . .

---

tioch and, as Acts confirms, had to travel further west hoping to find acceptance for his missionary preaching. Later he wrote to the Romans willing to modify his views but still maintaining his fundamental gospel. The tension between Jewish and Gentile/Christianity which had been present from the beginning of the Christian mission as reported in Acts was not resolved.

Thus Paul never preached to the Gentiles without this harassment from those who disputed his understanding of the gospel of Jesus Christ. He may have ended his career as an isolated figure whose theological insights and emphases were destined for decline in subsequent centuries.

Obviously the defeat of Paul at Antioch did not mean that Paul was eliminated from the memory of the church. He is a hero in Acts and his letters have come down to us as authentic testimony to his understanding of the Jesus tradition. He was surely remembered as an apostle, a missionary and a martyr for the faith. But it is the latter that is more remembered than his teachings. The dispute at Antioch meant that the interpretation of the faith other than that of Paul became normative. This is seen in particular in the portrayal of Paul in Acts.

Interpretations of Paul

Luke, in the Acts of the Apostles, replaces Paul, with his particular theological perspective in Galatians and in Romans, with Paul, the one who will compromise his view for the sake of the unity of the church and the church authorities in Jerusalem. He is pictured in Acts as a theologian who could give wholehearted approval to the apostolic decree. He is also pictured as the one who would dutifully return to Jerusalem and submit himself to the authorities there (Acts 21:20–26). This all fits into the final picture of Christianity as seen in the pastoral epistles (to which Paul's authority is attached!) and the seven Catholic epistles, as well as the writings commonly called "apostolic fathers." Christianity had become a system of doctrine and, especially, an ethical code more so than an acknowledgment of God's redemptive act in Jesus as primary.

We can even say that recollection of this unresolved dispute did not disappear with the composition of the canonical New Testament. Marcion, for example, seems to have justified his preference for Paul by referring to Paul's condemnation of Peter. For Marcion, Paul had the true Christianity rather than Peter. This view was also shared by the Valentinians who held that Paul was the superior apostle. Ultimately what happened was that those who favored Peter were thought to be those who were right, "orthodox." Evidence for this position may be found as early as Matthew 16:17–18 in which the evangelist intended to combat claims made on behalf of some other apostolic authority. Perhaps this combated the self-exaltation of Paul of his authority in Galatians 2:11–13. It seems that the apostolic decree with its emphasis on doctrine and ethics was followed along with salvation by grace through faith. The latter was not to be regarded as the touchstone of the Christian faith but rather the interpretation given by the Jerusalem church.

Paul the Victor

And so Paul lost in his effort to influence the theological mind of the early church. The church preserved his letters but often interpreted them in a way different from his intention and even added to his authority the pastoral epistles which were clearly different from the teachings of the early Paul.

He may have lost the battle but not the war. His writings in Galatians and Romans, in particular, continue to challenge the church to take into account the particular dimension of justification through faith alone.

Paul was not always the victor. Like Jeremiah he had his anguish, his sting in the flesh from which he prayed to be delivered (2 Cor 12:7–9); he had confidence in the moral coherence of the world, proclaimed the supreme sovereignty of God, had an ability to criticize what he believed was wrong, and maintained a bold conviction in hope. Even in his life, Paul lived by grace rather than by works. He boasted of his weakness, defeat and peril. Those who rejected his doctrine of grace also criticized his life as an apostle. The controversies recorded in his letters give ample evidence of these people in the early church. His theology was actually experienced in his own life. He served a crucified savior. He could not be a triumphant apostle of such a savior. The ultimate triumph would be of grace. Paul would await that alone.

It may be difficult for Christians in the last decades of the twentieth century to accept some of these ideas, especially Roman Catholics. Why were they not understood long ago? But in fact, they were, for they are in the New Testament. We need always to return to the Bible as classic and see it again. What is Christianity primarily: a doctrinal system and a code of ethics or a proclamation of salvation through faith and the grace of God? All will say both but which is primary? Since ultimately the church takes life on the local level, pastors and bishops and laity will have to answer those questions. The more careful study of both Galatians and Romans offers all the possibility to continue to allow the *mysterion* to take hold of us as we grow in our understanding and allow the grace of God to so envelop us that God becomes God for us and we experience that saving presence of grace.

STUDY QUESTIONS

1. If the triumphant Paul becomes less triumphant, how does this affect your thinking on Paul?

2. Does Paul help in living a Christian life as a follower of the crucified Jesus?

3. Paul seems to have changed his mind and was willing to accept some compromise. Is compromise a virtue?

4. Various approaches have always characterized Christianity. What might this mean for the contemporary church?

5. How is the code of ethics and the system of doctrine easier than the gospel of freedom? How is the gospel of freedom easier than the code of ethics and the system of doctrine? What is a member of the church to think and to do?

6. Should the positions of Peter and Paul always cause tension in the church? Which position seems to dominate today?

7. If unity is the value above all, how would this affect the ecumenical movement?

8. Defeat is not always an evil. What might this mean today in the contemporary church?

9. What has intrigued you, disturbed you, bothered you, encouraged you in this chapter?

Chapter 4

PAUL'S GOSPEL

Christians usually associate the word gospel, *euangelion*, with the four books in the New Testament called Matthew, Mark, Luke and John. In fact, the word and its use antedate these four faith documents about Jesus and has its origin in Paul. The apostle to the Gentiles used "gospel" or "evangelization" more than anyone else in the New Testament, and when other writers use the word, they seem to have taken it from him. Etymologically the word means "good news." Although we use it as a common religious term, such usage was not common in antiquity, either among Jews or among Greeks. It does appear on an inscription in connection with emperor worship: "The birthday of the god (emperor) was for the world the beginning of good news" (*euangelion* in the plural). Whether or not this usage influenced Paul and later Christian tradition is debatable. We do know that the word is not used in the plural in Christianity and that it refers more to the content of Paul's preaching than to the actual preaching.

The good news has its origin in God (1 Thes 2:2, 8–9; 2 Cor 11:7; Rom 1:1 etc.), but the content concerned Christ (1 Thes 3:2; Gal 1:7). For Paul, gospel summed up his preaching that Jesus was the risen Lord, offering salvation to all, Jew and Gentile. The good news brought the saving presence of God to humankind that liberated in the present and promised a wonderful future. Enthusiasm flowed from the preacher of the good news to those who accepted the gospel in faith (Gal 1:23). Just as Paul felt compelled to accept the Lord Jesus in his religious experience, he felt compelled to preach this Lord and willingly became a servant of the gospel (Phil 2:22). The great apostle of the Gentiles lived conscious of God's special grace calling him to preach, not to baptize (1 Cor 1:7). Calling others to listen and respond in faith as Paul had responded was sufficient for him.

EUANGELION IN GREEK USAGE

A technical term for news of victory.
Good fortune is contained in the word.
It effects salvation for the people.
It signals the offering of sacrifice.
The emperor proclaims *euangelion* in his birth, his accession, his decrees.

The gospel Paul preached among the Gentiles was no different from that which was preached by the other apostles before him (Gal 1:17). Each had experienced the Lord, and so only one gospel exists even if Paul was conscious of different theologies among these same apostles. When opponents preached a different gospel (Gal 1:7 or 2 Cor 11:4) Paul reacts strongly and condemns this other gospel because it does not offer the saving presence of God in freedom. Paul based his understanding of the Jesus tradition on a firm conviction that God had freely entered into human history in Jesus, and now humankind, Jew and Gentile, could experience salvation.

Paul experienced a radical change in his life because of his encounter with the risen Lord. The good news about Jesus also radicalized Paul, and he expected the same for all who believed. Those who hear this good news must also make a radical decision to respond. The good news is not just some helpful hints in living. Nor is it a way of life among many. The gospel of Jesus was decisive with power for salvation. The content of this gospel involved some knowledge, but not exclusively knowledge. The good news about Jesus has the power to transform human life. The event which brought about this radical change in human history involved the death and resurrection, but the event of the past continued to have power in the present. The knowledge revealed in the gospel opens people to the saving activity of God in a new way through Jesus. The revelatory aspect of the gospel remains important, but only if the actual knowledge gives way to a powerful experience of God in a person's life. The gospel has power.

For Paul the gospel is also *mysterion*. Often enough this Greek word becomes translated as "mystery" or "secret" in English, but neither word conveys adequately the Greek meaning. *Mysterion* is understanding which invites, envelops, entices, calls for ever deeper involvement. *Mysterion* means that we know and we understand and appreciate and make our own, but at the same time we never fully

understand or know or personalize in any total fashion. The gospel
invites participation, which brings about an eternal becoming in anyone who responds. The knowledge gives way to growth and development and faith and hope and love. Paul lives and dies as the steward
who dispenses the wealth of the *mysterion* (1 Cor 4:1), bringing both
Jews and Gentiles into a communion with God and with each other
through the life, death and resurrection of the one savior of all, Jesus
Christ.

> But we impart a mystery and hidden wisdom of God which
> God decreed before the ages for our glorification (1 Cor
> 2:7).

> Lo, I tell you a mystery. We shall not all sleep, but we shall
> all be changed (1 Cor 15:51).

> Lest you be wise in your own conceits, I want you to under-
> stand this mystery (Rom 11:25).

> Now to him who is able to strengthen you according to my
> gospel and the preaching of Jesus Christ, according to the
> revelation of the mystery which was kept secret for long ages
> (Rom 16:25).

The *mysterion*, which is the gospel, assures all that God has entered into human history in Jesus. God has banished the power of evil;
God has promised a better future; God has made the present worth
living; God offers a release from despair and meaninglessness and
cynicism and pessimism and all the negative elements that seem to
plague both the individual and the human race. Things need not be
always so, not in the present and surely not in the future, for the good
news of God in Jesus has brought liberation and freedom and peace
and reconciliation for all. No wonder Paul could throw himself into
his preaching. The radical and decisive event had taken place; now all
people had to do was to accept the grace offered and become transformed into new persons.

Paul's use of *mysterion* has some relationship to the word in the
mystery religions of the east, especially with regard to a participation
in the divine life. The fundamental ideas, however, are not from the
Greek mystery religions but from Old Testament and Jewish sources.
The word in Qumran literature conveys the hidden meaning of the
Old Testament, or the revelation that has taken place in Israel, not

---

MYSTERION IN GREEK USAGE

Cultic rites promising a sharing in the fate of the gods.

Secret knowledge and actions.

Sanctifying union with the gods and salvation.

Initiation of the elect into the sorrows and joys of the gods.

Promise of future hope.

---

primarily in the sense of knowledge but in the sense of the revelation that God has entered into a relationship with Israel and the people have responded. The combination of relationship with God and being continually drawn into the very communion with God explains sufficiently the gospel as *mysterion*.

The gospel as power proclaims that God has raised up Jesus from the dead. The gospel lives powerfully, not as empty words but as the great deed that confounds all that the power of evil can demonstrate. Jesus lives. People can look to eternal life, delivered from the coming wrath (1 Thes 1:10), and thus this good news has come to us "with power and the Holy Spirit" (1 Thes 1:5). Paul knew that the power of the gospel had changed his life and had changed the lives of those who listened to him in faith and accepted the gospel of God about Jesus. The world was different, people were different, the power was unleashed and flowed out over all humankind, affecting the very planet. Humankind needed to believe in this gospel of salvation bestowed on people as a gift of God's grace, not as a reward of merit but all through faith in Jesus. "All have sinned and fall short of the glory of God" (Rom 3:23). All needed the saving presence of the one God.

Salvation for All

Salvation for Jew and Gentile rests not upon ethical achievement but on the grace of God. Both need to have their past offenses blotted out by an act of divine mercy and to have the assurance of acceptance by God only on the spontaneous forgiveness of a gracious God. God accepts all believers, whether Jew or Gentile, as righteous. With this justification in the presence of God also comes peace, joy and the hope of future glory. Above all, believers receive the Holy Spirit, who empowers them to endure all for the sake of the gospel.

Now people live a new life. Sin no longer has any power, for the believer has been freed from its control. Where once death came as a result of sin and alienation from God, now eternal life becomes the destiny of those who have made their commitment in faith. This, however, does not imply that all believers are forever free from sinning. Paul knows too well the weakness of human nature. For the apostle to the Gentiles, the failure of believers to always live up to their new lives only allows God to continue to be gracious and forgiving. God loves not because people do not sin but even when people sin.

Paul the Jew also believes in freedom from the law. Under the Jewish law people lived in a state of tension. They knew what was right, but another power worked within: the power of sin, which compelled people to act contrary to what was known to be right. "I of myself serve the law of God with my mind, but with my flesh I serve the law of sin" (Rom 7:25b). Salvation through faith delivers people from law, for now grace abounds instead of people relying on their own efforts.

The One Gospel

What Paul preached remains a constant guide for all subsequent generations of believers. No other gospel exists (Gal 1:7). The cornerstone of this gospel, justification by God, can cause problems for all believers, often enough in particular Christian leaders. Such "uneasiness" about what Paul preached, however, can never deny the rightful place of what Paul gave his life to preserve. When certain Judaizing practices were being foisted on Gentiles in the early church, Paul reacted strongly. The gospel brings freedom (Gal 2:4) which must be preserved in the presence of any efforts to confine or limit. Even Peter received the rebuke of Paul when in Paul's mind he no longer walked according to the true gospel (Gal 2:14). Paul preached a liberal interpretation of the Jesus tradition, especially when compared to the more conservative approach of the Jewish Christian community associated with James and Jerusalem. He would not tolerate any burden being laid uselessly upon the back of any believer, for the good news liberated and made one free.

In Jesus, God had proclaimed his presence to the human race, and no person of any position even within the apostolic church could prevent the power of God from working in the lives of individual believers. Paul believed that left alone all are worthy of the wrath of God (Rom 1:18), but all are delivered from the wrath of God through Jesus and now stand justified in the presence of God. The one gospel continues to offer people of every age a sense of deliverance and enthusiastic freedom. All are saved, "everyone who has faith, the Jew first and also the Greek" (Rom 1:16).

Crucified and Risen

Frequently Paul focuses on the risen Lord as the heart of his gospel (1 Thes 1:10; Rom 10:9). In 1 Corinthians 2:2, he mentions only the cross: "I decided to know nothing among you except Jesus Christ and him crucified." For Paul, cross and resurrection constitute a single event which manifests the power of God for goodness. He will emphasize one or the other depending upon the context. Perhaps this is most clear in his statement: "Christ died for our sins and rose for our justification" (Rom 4:25). No resurrection without crucifixion and, with gratitude to God, no crucifixion without resurrection. Perhaps some will want to focus more on the resurrection than on its prior moment, the death of the Lord. Paul will not accept such a possibility. His gospel finds its foundation on the death of the Lord.

At the time of Jesus, the Jews did not expect a suffering messiah. All of the efforts on the part of Christians to find clear prophecies in the Old Testament on the suffering servant and then applying this to the messiah may make eminent sense to Christians but made no sense to Jews. The messiah should not suffer and die. No wonder that many Jews had trouble accepting Jesus as the messiah. For Paul, the messiah not only suffered and died but he had to do so, for, in dying, Jesus effectively conquered sin. How Jesus and his death conquered sin has raised questions for Christians for centuries. Paul himself struggled with the idea and came up with his conclusion: the death of Jesus did not change the attitude of God by turning away God's wrath, but rather deals with humanity and sin. Now people can rely on God alone and on God's grace.

Redemption/Expiation

In Romans, Paul used traditional language and wrote: "They are justified by his grace as a gift, through the redemption which is in

---

PARADIDOMAI

Mt 4:12 hearing that John had been handed over

Mt 10:4 Judas Iscariot who handed him over

Mk 13:9 they will hand you over to the Sanhedrin

Lk 1:2 just as they were handed over to us

Jn 6:64 who it was who should hand him over

Acts 3:13 Jesus, whom you handed over

Rom 1:24 God handed them over into the lusts of their hearts

1 Cor 11:2 as I handed over to you the traditions (*paradoseis*)

Christ Jesus, whom God put forward as an expiation by his blood to be received by faith" (Rom 3:24–25). The Greek word for expiation (*hilasterion*) can also be translated "mercy seat," an allusion to the top of the ark of the covenant in the temple in Jerusalem. On the day of atonement, the top of the ark was sprinkled with blood from the sacrifice which signified in ritual that God had granted forgiveness. The word does not mean propitiation, which could imply that somehow the attitude of God was changed and the wrath was dissolved. Rather, an expiation actually takes away sin instead of appeasing a wronged God. God does not have a problem with sin; humanity has the problem. The same idea is present with the idea of dying for our sins and rising for our justification (Rom 4:25). The Greek word here, *paradidomai*, means "to hand over," the same word used in the Lord's supper tradition (1 Cor 11:23). Instead of being "betrayed" by Judas, the better translation seems to be handed over by God.

For a change to take place in humanity, God handed over Jesus to death; the power of evil was granted the possibility of destroying Jesus forever, but God would not allow the goodness of his Christ to be destroyed and so God raised him up: "While we were still sinners Christ died for us" (Rom 5:8). This understanding of God and Jesus and sin and death and resurrection forms the foundation of the gospel preached by Paul.

PAUL'S TEACHING

1. God overcomes the power of evil by raising Jesus from the dead.
2. Sin, which estranges people from God, is conquered in the death and resurrection.
3. God used the death of Jesus to bring about the new relationship with humanity.
4. This relationship is based not upon a change in God but upon a change in humanity.
5. The love of Jesus for humanity and the love of God for Jesus and humanity led Jesus to the cross.
6. God did not demand the death of Jesus to appease wrath but delivered him up to the power of evil in death so that God could defy evil and death by raising Jesus from the dead.
7. Since Jesus died because of the sins of humanity, as risen, he has affected a new relationship with God for all humanity. People are justified.
8. God offers salvation to all through faith based not on merit, but on the gracious will of a loving creator.
9. People can stand in God's presence with dignity not because of what they do or not do, but solely because of God's gift.
10. Faith in Jesus brings salvation.

How much Paul personally formulated his ideas and how much was dependent upon what he had received remains unknown. We have the witness of his gospel, which is sufficient. All are being drawn into the great mystery disclosed by God in Jesus. The gospel is not a once-and-for-all understanding for everyone. Rather, believers are caught up into a vortex which is God, and in that vortex all are influenced and affected and are invited into a never-ending spiral of activity, the power and goodness of God in Christ Jesus. No wonder Paul can claim that nothing we could ever do would ever merit such a justification.

Paul Preaches His Gospel

Paul understood his gospel in the light of his Judaism. He also experienced a sense of liberation and freedom that compelled him to enthusiastically proclaim to others what he had experienced. The gospel he preached at first glance seems so easy: God has saved all, and people need only to believe. In fact, the gospel, although freeing, also demands. If people are different, if God has graciously changed humanity and invited all into a loving relationship, then people should live according to their new state. The gospel offers hope and gives encouragement; it promises eternal life. People who have been so blessed should live that blessing. Only then can the one gospel lived and preached by Paul take root in the minds and hearts and lives of people.

With this as a foundation, we can now turn to the actual words of Paul as he deals with the preaching of the gospel to the Gentiles. With a knowledge of his personality, his religious experience, his historical situation and a general sense of what he preached, contemporary believers can read Galatians and Romans and experience the power of the faith of the great apostle to the Gentiles.

STUDY QUESTIONS

1. There is only one gospel, one good news, but many interpretations of this good news. What is so interesting or unusual about Paul's interpretation of the Jesus tradition?

2. The gospel radicalized Paul. Does this still happen? What might this mean today?

3. Mystery means ever fuller understanding. How has this been true in the study of the Jesus tradition, in the study of Paul?

4. Salvation is God's gift. How does this become real for believers today?

5. Do some people have trouble with the idea of salvation as a gift, rather than something earned?

6. Salvation seems to demand suffering. Does suffering make any sense? Are people supposed to be suspended from some mystical cross?

7. How could someone summarize the conclusions of Paul's gospel? What is your reaction to these ideas?

8. The gospel frees. The gospel demands. Does this imply a contradiction?

SECTION II

The Epistle to the Galatians

Chapter 5

INTRODUCTION TO GALATIANS

The Origin of the Letter to the Galatians

The letter of Paul to the Romans causes no problems in identifying those addressed: Jewish Christians living in Rome. The letter to the Galatians, however, raises several questions: Who were the people addressed? What part of Asia did they occupy? What was the ethnic, social and cultural situation of the churches addressed? Definitive answers to these questions are unattainable presently and perhaps will always be so. Contemporary scholars can provide only some suggestions.

Many will point to the central plateau of Asia Minor as the territory. Some will trace the Galatians to the Celtic tribes who in the third century before Christ pushed into the Balkans and settled around Ancyra. Subsequent careful maneuvering by these tribes brought official favor from Rome, and in 25 B.C. Augustus created the Roman province of Galatia which included the earlier territory around Ancyra as well as parts of Pisidia, Pamphylia, and Lycaonia. Culturally the tribes adapted quickly, first to Greek and then to Roman customs and practice, but they also maintained some Celtic cultural practices, especially in rural areas. Such acculturation flourished primarily among the aristocratic and wealthy class. Whether the Galatians to whom Paul writes were direct descendants of the original cults or the multi-ethnic mixture found in most Hellenistic-Roman towns we do not know. Perhaps they were.

From the tone of the letter and its careful composition many have concluded that the recipients were well-educated people with some financial means. Paul's listeners made significant changes in their lives as a result of his preaching: they stopped worshiping the pagan

MAP OF GALATIA

gods (4:8–10), moved from polytheists to monotheists, especially in their worship and prayers (3:20; 4:6), and eliminated all distinctions (3:28). Paul's gospel of freedom involved a religious, social and political experience. The Galatians accepted it readily and probably were pleased that he considered them adults in this new way of living (4:1–3).

Readers should note that Paul refers to "churches" (1:2). Where these communities were actually located may remain forever in shadows, but the majority of contemporary scholars locate them in central Anatolia, which would be modern central Turkey. When Paul founded these churches also remains unknown. We may try to resolve some of these questions by referring to Acts, but as we have learned, Luke cannot be relied upon for completely accurate information. We can conclude that Paul founded various communities in what is now central and southern Turkey and that these churches were predominantly Gentile, perhaps with some historical roots to the Celts of some three and a half centuries before. They were probably well educated and were not identified with the poorer classes.

An important element in the understanding of the letter involves some who were opposed to Paul and his teaching. They seemed to have caused the situation which occasioned the letter. Without addressing his opponents directly, Paul deals with the issues they raised. It seems that these antagonists had pressured the members of these churches to accept the Torah and circumcision. They contacted the churches in Galatia after Paul had founded them and apparently had left. They preached "another gospel" (1:6–9) and had some connection with the Jerusalem church and with James and were part of the debate about the requirements for acceptance into the Christian community (2:4–5, 11–14). Apparently these opponents were Jewish Christian missionaries rivaling Paul and his missionary activity. Other than the relationship to Judaism, they probably preached the same gospel as Paul and were sincere in their efforts to respond to the needs of the Galatian churches. These Gentile Christians in Galatia, in turn, seem to have accepted willingly what the missionaries from Jerusalem preached. In so doing, they incurred the wrath of Paul.

Since these church communities had educated membership we cannot ascribe their change to mere foolishness, as Paul does (3:1). In all probability, they had responded enthusiastically to Paul and his preaching and then with the passage of time had to try to settle other issues to which the "freer" gospel of Paul did not give easy answers. They then had the experience of other Christian missionaries who must have impressed them sufficiently so that their interpretation of the Jesus tradition, especially in relationship to Judaism, was accepted. It may very well be that these believers in Galatia had the problem of trying to reconcile the gospel of justification through faith alone with the daily problems of life. How do people filled with the Spirit of God, already reconciled to God, deal with daily sin?

Torah, law and observance help people to deal with daily sins. They can strive to observe the law and remove themselves from all defilement and thus can stand worthily as sons and daughters in the presence of God. They will become part of the covenant and can be assured of their salvation through their observance of the covenantal law. In the eyes of the opponents of Paul, to be free from the law made people slaves of sin, and even Christ himself would be a servant of sin (2:17). Compared to the very general ideas of faith, grace and justification, these opponents of Paul offered definite ways to obtain God's favor and to live in God's favor. They needed a law to tell them what was right or wrong, and the opponents of Paul offered such a law. They needed a ritual to overcome transgressions and received that as well from the opponents of Paul. Left only with the Spirit and freedom, how could people live securely in an evil world and with the evils of people, especially the evils within the flesh (5:13, 16, 17, 19; 6:12, 13)? Transgressions had to happen, and then what? No wonder the churches of Galatia accepted the law of circumcision and all the security it brought.

Date of the Letter

Galatians was certainly written before Romans. As we shall see, Paul changes his tone considerably after he loses his support in Galatia. Since Romans was possibly Paul's last letter, probably sent from Corinth before his final journey to Jerusalem, it would help if we could determine the relationship between Galatians and other Pauline letters, but this is not possible. We can end up only with an approximate dating. Since this letter seems to belong to the earlier part of his difficulties with opponents from Jewish Christianity, the most likely date would fall between 50 and 55 and probably closer to 55.

From where it was written is also unknown. Most scholars favor Ephesus. Corinth and Macedonia are also possibilities. The form itself is apologetic, with rhetorical elements within a general framework of a letter of the period. It begins with a prescript, including a doxology (1:5). The body of the letter contains an exhortation with a narrative

Opponents	Paul
law	freedom
circumcision	no circumcision
law makes people worthy	God makes people worthy
freedom from law makes people slaves of sin	law enslaves
ritual overcomes sin	God overcomes sin

(1:6–2:14), a proposition and proof (2:15–4:31), with warnings and recommendations (5:1–6:10). The epistle concludes with a postscript (6:11–18).

The letter was written to respond to a particular need in the mind of Paul. It has, however, in history become a letter as part of the New Testament canon. We will never be able to fully understand its importance for Paul, for the churches at Galatia, or for the early development of Christianity. We must settle for some significant approaches to Christianity as understood by Paul and then try to make the necessary adaptations to the Christianity of today. What Paul intended as an occasional letter has ultimately become an expression of faith recognized by the early church as authentically expressing the faith of the community.

GALATIANS

I. Introduction (1:1–11)

II. Narration: Paul's call and his gospel (1:12–2:21)

III. Explanation of his gospel (3:1–4:31)

IV. Closing exhortation to Christian living (5:1–6:10)

V. Postscript: farewell and blessing (6:11–18)

STUDY QUESTIONS

1. How can some knowledge of the recipients help in understanding the letter of Paul to the Galatians?

2. Why would Gentiles find the law of Judaism appealing? Why would the law cause problems?

3. Is it difficult to reconcile the freeing gospel to life today? What are the implications?

4. Law is good. Law is bad. How is law part of life and Christianity?

Chapter 6

PAUL AND HIS GOSPEL

Suggested Scriptural Reading:

Galatians 1-2

Introduction to the Letter (1:1-11)

The opening of Galatians clearly attests to the author and its literary form as a letter. Paul writes an occasional letter to some churches in what he calls Galatia. In an unusual manner, however, the very style hints at problems. Paul asserts strongly that his apostleship is from God, through Jesus whom God has raised. He writes to churches which evidently are geographically close, offering grace and peace. These wishes are common in his letters but usually the opening ends with a thanksgiving. Here no thanksgiving is offered since he will not know if a thanksgiving is due until his recipients have responded.

The conclusion of the greeting sets the stage for what follows: Christ gave himself up for our sins (1:4) and thus, as will become evident, his redeeming act is sufficient for all. Since Christ died for our sins, we need no longer give notice to them. Paul begins by stating clearly that Christ and his death is sufficient for redemption with no exception.

Where we would expect a thanksgiving or a word of affirmation about his readers, Paul follows with an accusation: they are abandoning the gospel (1:6). He follows by arguing for the authority of the gospel he has preached. The message of grace and freedom has been questioned and Paul rises to defend what he has preached. For Paul this one gospel has the supreme authority, and all else, leadership, ministry, position, doctrine and moral encouragement, must flow from the fundamental gospel of grace. This one gospel proclaims

Jesus as the one liberator from all oppression. This one gospel is God's activity drawing people into the realm of God's grace (1:6–7). No one in heaven or on earth can supplant this fundamental activity of God in Christ Jesus. What God has established will prevail.

Paul, Called To Preach (1:12–2:14)

This section of Galatians deals with Paul's personal history as an apostle. Many have tried to carefully relate this to the account in Acts to no avail. As we have already seen, readers should pay more attention to what Paul has to say in his own letters than what Luke writes in Acts when seeking historicity. We have already seen something of the scenario that is followed in this commentary. After his conversion experience, Paul goes to Arabia. What he did and why he went there is not recorded and need not be the ground for speculation. He did not go to Jerusalem to get approval for his mission; the risen Lord had already given him that. Rather, Paul was concerned about church unity and wanted to be sure that the Christian community could be united even if it was composed of different groups. The only request made to the Gentiles was to remember the poor (1:10). This Paul would gladly preach. By the time he resumed his preaching, other requirements were laid upon the Gentiles. To this Paul objected.

Paul was anxious to establish his relationship with the Jerusalem apostles and wanted to maintain the unity so much needed in early Christianity as it began to develop into a Jewish and Gentile church. He also wanted to demonstrate the power of the gospel which could turn a zealot against Christianity to a zealot for Christianity. God chose him, called him, revealed his Son to Paul and sent him to the Gentiles (1:15–16). His conversion was more a call to ministry, for Paul to explain the love of God for all, even those marginally-religious types called Gentiles. From Paul the Pharisee, such a change appeared revolutionary. No wonder people wondered about the one who had set out to destroy the faith and then became the preacher (1:23–24).

The second meeting in Jerusalem (2:1–10) deals with both theology and history. For Paul to include this meeting in the context of his letter to the Galatians must have meant more than just some autobiographical detail. The early church no doubt struggled with the question of Jewish Christian and Gentile Christian relations. Often enough the two groups must have come close to a breaking point but somehow unity had to be preserved. There is one church. And Paul the apostle to the Gentiles saw the unity of the church resting upon the one gospel of grace. Paul went to present to the Jerusalem church the message he was preaching so that he would not run in vain (2:2). He did not desire an authorization for what he preached but rather wanted to know if they all had the same understanding of what the gospel meant. Paul would not want two understandings of the gospel of Jesus, one for Jews and another for Gentiles. He did not want to start a new church but clearly would have to deal boldly with a mentality which saw preaching first to the Jews and only then to the Gentiles as well as a mentality which expected Gentiles to first become Jews.

The reference to Titus also clarifies Paul's unity with the Jerusalem church. Some had wanted Titus, a Gentile, to be circumcised, but for Paul this would be contrary to the gospel of grace, and the Jerusalem pillars (James, Cephas and John 2:9) gave him the hand of fellowship and acknowledged that he would preach to the Gentiles (2:9).

The unity of the church will rest upon the one gospel of grace in the midst of great diversity. Paul might have decided to avoid the whole question of relationship to the Jerusalem community but rather chose to seek their understanding and their support for the sake of the church. The unity of the one gospel also expected a unity that could be expressed among many peoples. The diversity could enhance the unity and need not destroy it. For Jews to become Christians meant that they could carry with them the best of their Jewish traditions and incorporate them into their new understanding of God and grace. For Gentiles, no need existed for them to include in their understanding of God the traditions of Judaism.

The change alluded to in 2:11–14 has already been mentioned. The accord reached in Jerusalem was quickly challenged and additional requirements were to be expected of Gentiles. All seemed to agree that circumcision was not required, but what of other Jewish traditions? Paul acknowledges that he confronted Peter, and the reason had to be the same as his intention to go to Jerusalem: the unity of the church based upon the gospel of grace and freedom. This issue, which also was the issue facing the Galatians, was included in the letter to bolster Paul's position.

Why did Peter, Barnabas and other Jewish Christians stop eating with Gentile Christians? The setting is Antioch. At first, Gentiles evidently were not only welcome into the church but also joined with Jewish Christians in common meals (eucharist?). Then suddenly after some people from James arrived, Peter noticeably withdrew and then, along with him, other Jewish Christians. For Paul this was a

---

UPOKRISIS IN GREEK USAGE

origin of the English word hypocritical

insincerity or lack of principle

apostasy or defiance of God

---

failure to understand the gospel. No one need become a Jew before becoming a Christian, and so Gentile Christians and Jewish Christians can eat together (2:14).

From our vantage point it may seem cowardly of Peter and the others to withdraw from table fellowship, but perhaps more was involved than meets the eye. At this time of great Jewish nationalism, many Jews wanted to separate themselves from any contact with the Gentiles. Jewish Christians who had yet to break completely with the synagogue had to live in the midst of a somewhat hostile Jewish community, and any hint of contact with the Gentiles might have caused even greater problems for the Jerusalem Christian community. Peter may have withdrawn to save further problems for the Jerusalem church. Though Peter might have withdrawn to lessen problems, he created more as far as Paul was concerned. Peter thus may not have acted out of lack of conviction or hypocritically (2:13) but rather out of his concern for the greater good of the Jewish Christian community at Jerusalem. No matter what the reason, such lack of unity with Gentile Christians proved unacceptable to Paul. Peter and the others were "apostates" abandoning the true meaning of the gospel of grace and freedom and instead were relying on law.

Paul includes the incident to emphasize the grace of the gospel, and the Galatians are accountable to that first and not to anyone who presents a different authority. Like Paul himself, the Galatians should resist giving up the gospel of grace. Paul saw unity coming from the gospel and not from some observance of Jewish traditions. This serves as a transition to the fundamental theme of the letter: justification by faith.

Paul's Presentation of the Gospel (2:15–21)

In 2:15–21 Paul moves from history and personal narrative to his theology of grace. Paul switches from "you" to "we." Here he and

Peter agree that people need to be set in a right relationship to God, need to be declared blameless. For Paul, only Jesus can do this and not any law. Almost responding to a question (2:17) Paul declares that sin is not measured by the failure to obey a law but by the failure to believe and accept Christ and his death as a saving act of God for all. Clinging to law as a standard makes Christians become sinners which Paul can no longer accept (2:18).

In verse 18 Paul changes from "we" to "I." At first some may interpret this as personal to Paul, and thus he becomes pious in his affirmation of personal mysticism. But on the contrary the "I" is meant to be universal and apply to everyone. All can say: it is no longer "I" who live but Christ who lives in me (2:20). Believers are included in the death of Christ even though it happened at a particular moment of time. Verses 19–21 climax the argument: Christ's death has made a new life possible, bringing freedom and grace. The person responds in faith alone. To imply that anything else could possibly bring about this new life is tantamount to sin for Paul.

People have a choice: works or faith. Paul states that salvation comes from faith. For if "justification were through law, then Christ died to no purpose" (2:21). People respond to the faith of Christ with the emphasis on Christ's faith or faithfulness rather than the human reaction of faith in Christ. Jesus remained faithful in obedience unto death. Thus God's declaration of grace has freed humanity from law. People cannot save themselves by observance but only by responding in faith to the faith of Christ.

This passage introduces for the first time "justification by faith," a rallying cry of the reformation. Since Paul is dealing here in the social context of Jews and Gentiles, he first declares that God's favorable judgment in Christ means that Gentiles are included just as Jews are included with no difference. Accepting God's judgment of not guilty means the acceptance of all people, even those with different backgrounds such as Gentiles. Thus Peter and others can eat with them. God justifies to unite and unites to justify.

God continues his activity in the individual who has been justified by sanctifying. In verses 15–21 the word justification appears four times emphasizing the forensic dimension of God's activity. Sinners are set in a new relationship. It is a gift which is received as a gift. The people are freed from slavery under the law and now serve the Lord in freedom. "Christ lives in them." Now the believer continues to live as crucified with Christ as a daily experience and experiences both justification and sanctification.

Paul responded to the problem of how God saves people in Galatians by affirming that God does so through the crucified Christ and people respond in faith. But then salvation also means living under the reign of God. Justification is not only a gift but a responsibility. It involves living with others in a community of faith, with people who live for each other, even with people who are different. Previously significant differences are gone. Now people live a life of the justified and as unified.

STUDY QUESTIONS

1. Paul seems to begin his letter in a nasty way. How does this fit your understanding of his personality? His understanding of the gospel?

2. Paul defends his gospel and his apostleship. Why would this be necessary? Why does he have problems with the Jerusalem church?

3. Unity is important but differences can also enhance—so thinks Paul. How can this be understood today?

4. What image do you have of Peter? Does Paul seem more appealing than Peter or Peter more appealing than Paul?

5. What does sin mean today, for Paul, for the church, for the world?

6. Does doing good works make people feel more comfortable with God?

7. What does justification by faith mean personally?

Chapter 7

SALVATION BY FAITH

Suggested Scriptural Reading:

Galatians 3–4

The Experience of the Spirit (3:1–5)

Accepting Gentiles into full communion into the people of God might involve politics and sociological or psychological or historical elements, but ultimately Gentiles' full communion is theological. Paul knew this and tried to convince others, including the pillars of the Jerusalem church. When he turned to the Galatians he wanted to remind them what his preaching meant and how they responded and its effects.

He begins by calling them "foolish." Within three verses he uses the word "foolish" twice. The contemporary reader should not be shocked by such language. It was rather common in diatribes in Paul's day. The Galatians would not have been as insulted as a contemporary believer. Still, the point is clear. He begins with a harsh address. The question rises: Does the Spirit come as a result of the law or by faith (3:2)? The answer is obvious because the Galatians were not under the law at the beginning of their Christian life, nor according to Paul are they really law observers now. God gave them the Spirit. They experienced a sense of enthusiasm and experienced miracles (3:5) as a result of Paul's preaching of Christ crucified and not from any observance of the law. The proclamation of Christian faith is sufficient for God's grace and therefore sufficient for the Galatians. Thus, Paul thinks they are foolish. If they had enough sense just to ask themselves who they were and what they were before the law, they would know the answer themselves.

Unfortunately they have been bewitched by some who think that observance ensures God's favor. But no special rites nor religious observances validate the presence of the Spirit. God gives the Spirit freely. The Spirit, used here for the first time in this letter, implies God's presence and power operative in the world and the new community. This Spirit comes as a result of the preaching of the crucified Jesus and not from any effort to gain God's favor through obedience to the law.

Paul contrasts the Spirit with "flesh." The usage here is puzzling. It only makes sense when one lives as moving from flesh to Spirit and not the other way around. The Galatians had already experienced the Spirit and now they are relying on the "flesh," in particular the rite of circumcision. Paul sees such thinking as complete foolishness. Equally absurd is believing that the gift of the Spirit is somehow imperfect to be made perfect through the observance of the law of circumcision, doing something to "flesh."

Paul seems to have reached the end of his wits. "Have you experienced such things in vain" (3:4)? If they think that all he said about grace and faith must be supported now by law and circumcision, then in fact he did preach in vain. Paul, however, does not believe this, for he has chosen to write to them to shock them back into living as they had already lived before they were troubled by others preaching a different gospel.

Paul concludes with his first argument: Has God responded to the Galatians because of law or because of faith (3:5)? He used a question knowing that the Galatians must respond affirmatively and thus support Paul's argument. God has granted the Spirit to the Galatians as a gift. Since the Spirit continues to work among them, then God is still present with them. The answer is obvious. Salvation, the presence of the Spirit of God, comes through faith alone and not through the observance of the law.

The Argument from Scripture (3:6–14)

Who are the people of God? This question still troubles Christians today. In the past some Christians have excluded Jews from being the people of God in favor of Christians. Others quickly say both Jews and Christians or just everyone. The debate existed in early Christianity as well. Paul responded by simply saying that faith distinguished the true followers of Abraham and thus faith makes a person a member of God's people.

Eventually Christianity split from Judaism. Exactly when this

Verses 6–9 introduce Abraham and quote two Old Testament quotations associated with him.

Verses 10–12 quote Deuteronomy 27:26 and Habakkuk 2:4 to show that the law can never do for them what they need.

In verses 13–14 Christ represents the guilty and they go free.

happened is not clear. Certainly by the end of the century Christianity was on its own but the separation began long before. With the entrance of Gentiles into the church several questions needed to be determined. Who makes up the people of God? Who are Abraham's descendants? What is the place of law in the community of God? How does Judaism fit in?

Paul knows his answer but turns to the Old Testament to confront the very people who claim to be living according to the law. In these few verses Paul quotes the Pentateuch five times and Habakkuk once. By so doing Paul implies that these foolish Galatians who want to be under the law do not even hear the law.

The arguments are not easy to follow, especially since Paul seems to draw conclusions from the texts which are not so evident. The general direction of Paul's argument, however, remains clear: in Christ Jesus the blessings of Abraham have been given to the Gentiles so that they might receive the promised Spirit through faith (3:14).

His logic is clear even if at times a reader can get lost in the words. God reckoned his righteousness to Abraham by faith (Gen 15:6). Thus faith distinguishes the true descendants of Abraham. The family of Abraham, and thus of God, is made up of people of faith and not joined by any natural genealogy or through some observance of law. Abraham is the father of all the nations who accept God's grace in faith.

Paul does not wish to deny the roots of Christianity nor his own roots. Jesus was a Jew and lived and died as a Jew and therefore he is to be understood only in the context of Judaism. That Gentiles are now part of this new community is a testimony to the faithfulness of God as witnessed in Genesis 12:3: "In you shall all the nations be blessed." God has promised Abraham and God has remained true to his promise.

When Paul uses the word law (nomos) sometimes it is hard to specify what he means. It can mean the Mosaic law or the Pentateuch without distinguishing the legal and non-legal material. It also may

---

NOMOS

- What is proper.

- An accepted norm, order, custom, usage, tradition.

- Legal norms.

- What is valid in social dealings.

- Norm of life in the city (*polis*).

- The will and person of the king.

- Legal writings of the Old Testament.

- The word of God for the Jews.

- The Torah (teaching, instruction, revelation).

---

mean the Old Testament as a whole. In addition "law" may also mean a particular law or norm or principle to be observed.

In trying to explain the "law" Paul means the whole Pentateuch in these verses and argues that the Torah (law or Pentateuch) does not imply two ways of salvation, one through a person's observance of laws and the other through the power of God. For the true observer of the law knows that the law does not bring salvation, and so this person puts trust in the faithfulness of God alone. Paul interpreted Torah as who the Jews are rather than what the Jews do. Paul accepts the Torah as beginning the story of God's relationship with people to be completed in the death and resurrection of Jesus. This aspect of the "law" makes eminent sense to Paul but not the law that requires people to do or not to do. Torah continues to have meaning in the coming of Jesus but only as the preliminary aspect of God's gracious will for people.

Christ the innocent one became accursed so that the accused might become exonerated. He shared in the human condition including a degrading death and thus accomplished redemption for all. But what exactly does Paul mean by the "curse of the law" (3:10)? What value is the law if the curse falls on those who rely on their own fulfillment of the law, which is sin, and on those who fail to keep the whole law? All of Judaism is included. Nor does he exclude Gentiles, for they are outside the law and are cursed by the law's exclusiveness. The "us" whom Christ redeems then is both Gentiles and Jews together. The curse has become a blessing. Those who think they can make it on their own, those who do not even try and those who are outside are all united in the one redemptive act of Jesus. Death by crucifixion which for Jews connoted ignominy and scandal (Deut 21:23) becomes the means by which God fulfills his promises for all. Now all are united, Jew and Gentile, pious and impious, saint and sinner.

The Law and Humanity (3:15–18)

The Torah had always been Israel's pride and joy. With it they were a people; without it they were alone. Temple could go, priesthood could die, but the Torah enabled Israel and Judaism to continue. If Paul has changed the meaning of the people of God he must also deal with the place of the Torah in this new understanding of God's relationship to people. He does so in verses 15–29.

In certain Jewish traditions Torah pre-existed the actual giving of the law to Moses. Torah, like wisdom and word and spirit, belonged properly to God and then found expression in human life. Paul does not accept this understanding of law. For him, Torah came with Moses and follows the promise made to Abraham. He wished to root his understanding of the law in a previous and, for him, more significant promise on the part of God to Abraham. God's fidelity shines more prominently than any law of Moses seems to underlie Paul's thought in these verses (15–18).

Once a testament has been ratified no one can add to or cancel it. Thus Paul begins. The promise made to Abraham is identical with the blessing, and this is the testament made by God. The argument seems clear to Paul: Abraham did not know the Torah, yet he was judged righteous by God. The revelation of the Torah four hundred and thirty years later (Paul is using the tallying from Ex 12:40) could never cancel the testimony of God made in promise to Abraham involving the blessing of the nations. Consequently nor can the Torah cancel Abraham's way of obtaining righteousness through faith. What was possible for Abraham before the Torah is also possible for all now through Christ without the Torah. People inherit the blessing and salvation and redemption through faith in Christ. Paul has introduced the word inheritance which for him means all the benefits of God's work of salvation. If Abraham were promised the inheritance without the Torah, then this had to be based on a gift of grace made to Abraham by God. The promise made to Abraham as a gift now becomes the present work of salvation by God in Christ. Through this promise of old, salvation comes to the Gentiles through one seed (3:16), Christ.

The Jewish Law (3:19–25)

Here Paul finally speaks of why God provided the law: "because of transgressions" (3:19). Law changed unconscious wrongdoing to deliberate disobedience. Law was custodial with power to enslave but never to liberate. Law limited all possibilities but one: the one accomplished by Christ alone.

Some have tried to translate *paidagogos* as one who continues to instruct, but after the coming of Christ people are no longer under a custodian (*paidagogas*) (3:25). The law acted and served a particular function leading up to Christ and ending with the advent of Christ. God's salvation comes through grace alone. Human performance, however good, in no way sets the conditions for grace. In the past the law could divide people: those who knew it and those who did not; those who kept it and those who failed. Now all is over. The law can no longer divide people nor can it threaten people. What is accomplished was to point the people of Israel in the right direction, toward Christ. Once Christ has come, the law is done.

Paul has reinterpreted the law as a narrative of God's relationship with people climaxing with Jesus. Now the Torah can be fulfilled in the entrance of all peoples into the community of God and living a life based on the love of God and neighbor interpreted in the light of the life, death and resurrection of Jesus. Love may not always give us the clearest of answers, especially to the most complicated questions, but it surely gives a direction. Paul's attitude is a firm conviction that all are blessed in Christ, both Jew and Gentile, as all barriers are taken down that separate peoples. If they follow who they are with a life based on love of each other, then peace and joy and freedom are inevitable conclusions for all.

Unity and Equality (3:26–29)

These four verses sum up what Paul hopes to teach. He was most concerned about unity, and this can be accomplished only through faith and equality. Paul did not want Christianity split into two branches, one Jewish and one Gentile. He traveled to Jerusalem to avoid this. He confronted Peter because he was afraid of a similar split. Based upon the gospel, the community had to be united as one. "For in Christ Jesus you are all sons of God through faith" (3:26). Since Christ is the seed of Abraham (3:16) the Galatians are "in Christ Jesus" (26), "baptized into Christ" (27), "have put on Christ" (27), are "one in Christ Jesus" (28), "belong to Christ" (29). Paul seems interested in the actual moment when an individual puts on Christ but bases his conviction on the actual Christ event when God reconciled the world to himself. Even if people were not aware of it, and Paul himself was not, God had reconciled humanity. The lordship of Christ is fact and baptism is when an individual is drawn into this event.

He concludes with his famous statement on equality: neither Jew nor Greek, slave nor free, male nor female. The three great divisions of ancient society lie buried with Christ in his death. Ethnic, social and sexual differences are gone inasmuch as they imply superiority or hostility. Such differences may continue to exist but in the eyes of God and his Christ they are irrelevant.

If God has so declared, then people must live with a sense of equality. For the problem of the Jewish Christian and Gentile Christian relationship, it is not sufficient that Gentiles be invited to membership in the family of God and excluded from social fellowship. One demands the other. Even the question of slavery receives a direction for the future if not in the time of Paul. We have done away with slavery but still struggle with Paul's almost revolutionary attitude toward the sexes. The church cannot be interested in the spiritual development of humankind and disinterested in the social needs. Paul the revolutionary wanted to emphasize the equality of the sexes before God, in the community and before each other.

The redefinition of the people of God is complete: Jews and Gentiles, slaves and free, male and female. All are one. Torah had separated Israel from other nations. In Christ the promise to Abraham has been fulfilled in that all nations are blessed. The people of God rest upon faith in Christ and is open to all. What follows is Paul's thought of what it means to be children of God with free access and the disastrous consequences if anyone would retreat to a way of life prior to the coming of Christ. For Paul the flirtation that the Galatians have enjoyed by being "bewitched" (3:10) must give way to a full understanding of who they are and their position as God's holy people in Christ through faith.

Heirs in Freedom (4:1–11)

Paul likes to use images in his writings. This we have already seen with his reference to the law as a guardian. He will use the image of a potter in Romans 10 and here he uses the image of a minor under the control of guardians or trustees. We should note, however, that Paul is not a writer of elevated prose. His images may be helpful but also can confuse, especially when he seems to switch his analogy. He begins with the idea of a child, an heir, waiting for the time when the inheritance can be received, and then switches to the idea of one adopted. Even though the images can become entangled, the idea seems clear: the law was useful for the child before the inheritance could be received but no longer when the one who was to be sent came to bring redemption (4:4).

Verse 3 offers a strange metaphor: when we were children we were slaves to the "elemental spirits of the universe." Some versions translate the Greek as "the basic principles of the world" (Jerusalem Bible). The key comes from verse 8, "you were in bondage to beings that by nature are no gods." Paul seems to accept the belief among pagans of fundamental forces or spirits which control human destiny and then says that if the Galatians accept circumcision and the demands of the law, they are once again submitting themselves to these forces and forfeiting the freedom that comes from faith in Christ. His comment however is that since these forces were useless and powerless in the past, "they are no gods," they are equally powerless now. Paul seems to equate the tendency of pagans to submit themselves to these useless spirits to the tradition of the Jews submitting themselves to the law. For him, both are powerless and of no use, especially when the gospel of freedom is an alternative.

The key figure in these verses is God who has sent his Son (verse 4). Paul has no interest or knowledge of the origins of Jesus other than that he was born of a woman, and since he also was born under the law, he was born a Jew. He situates him in the human family, in a particular moment of history, living under the historical conditions of Judaism. But then he continues. God sent Jesus to rescue those under the law, to release them from the bondage of law. He fulfills the promise that goodness will be preserved and evil will be destroyed, so that people will live as children and heirs. The elemental spirits of the universe are without power but God can give power to his Son Jesus to overcome all evil and bring redemption.

Finally the Spirit is given to assure the reality of this adoption. Now all who are in Christ can call upon God as "Abba." The Spirit functions to bring these adopted members into intimacy with the Father of the family, bringing a sense of security and an acceptance that, in fact, they really are God's children.

The use of the word "Abba" has special significance for the early church. It denotes a sense of intimacy and affection that would be reserved for a relationship within a family between a child and a loving parent. It carries familiarity and security and being comfortable in the presence of the parent. Jesus himself seems to have used the term in his life and in his need (Mk 14:36), and now all who have put on Christ can have the same type of intimate relationship with God. The Spirit which makes possible the calling of God "Abba" assures the Galatians that they are in fact sons, daughters and heirs and no longer slaves and outsiders. They belong.

With a noticeable sense of frustration Paul asks the Galatians, if all this is true, how they could possibly turn back and submit themselves to observances of days and seasons and months (4:10). All are foolish in light of what they have experienced as children of the one God whom they may call "Abba." They are turning back to the past which offered nothing (4:9). All that Paul hoped to accomplish for them seems lost (4:11), for they are more interested in serving strange elemental spirits (4:9) rather than enjoying the freedom of God's children.

An Appeal from Friendship (4:12–20)

But Paul has not given up. He has too much affection for the Galatians. He is their friend and they were all friends to him. In his need they responded and offered consolation and support and loving care (4:13–14). How can they turn against him now (4:16) when they were ready to give of their very selves to him when he preached among them (4:14–15)? He begs them to follow him in being free from the bondage of the law which only offers slavery (4:12).

Whatever his physical ailment was, Paul's readers knew well. They also knew how they responded in the past. For us, all we know is an appeal of the heart to ignore those who are trying to entice them to another gospel for the base motives of courting the favor of the Galatians (4:17–18).

The section ends with a mixture of metaphors in which the children once again are in the womb in need of being reborn. The point seems clear enough: Paul has given birth to them through his preaching, and now he thinks they once again must be released from the bondage of the womb to take their rightful place as God's children. The analogy fails, since Paul also thinks that Christ has given birth to them. Accepting false teaching has placed them in a pre-Pauline-preaching condition and they must once again be released so that Christ can be formed in them.

Paul draws his conclusion with a manifestation of his personal pain. They have been his charges and things have not gone well. Now he just wants to set things right again (4:19–20). He has spoken from his heart and wants only the best for the Galatians and wants them to experience what he has experienced in Christ Jesus (4:12).

The Children of the Free Woman (4:21–31)

After his emotional appeal in the previous section, the allegorical interpretation of Genesis seems to leave readers cold. Has not Paul said enough? Even his efforts to explain seem to lack clarity and often cause more problems than those that existed before he started. If these verses show anything, they demonstrate the extent to which Paul will go to emphasize the free grace of God. Paul wants the Galatians to see themselves as children of Sarah and thus of the promise. They must live as free children of the promise and resist any pressure to enslave themselves under any law.

Paul has already told his readers that a careful and true reading of the Torah would bring them to seeing its incompletion and imperfection to be completed and perfected in Christ (3:6–14). And so he begins with his rhetorical question (4:21). The allegory itself is taken from Genesis 21:9–12.

> But Sarah saw the son of Hagar the Egyptian whom she had borne to Abraham, playing with her son Isaac. So she said to Abraham: "Cast out this slave woman with her son; for the son of this slave woman shall not be heir with my son Isaac." And the thing was very displeasing to Abraham on account of his son. But God said to Abraham: "Do not be displeased because of the lad and because of your slave woman; whatever Sarah says to you, do as she tells you, for through Isaac shall your descendants be named."

The two sons of Abraham and their mothers are linked to Mount Sinai (Haggar and Ishmael) (4:24–25) and to the heavenly Jerusalem (Sarah and Isaac) (4:26–27). Ishmael is born according to ordinary circumstances while the true heir is born according to the power of God. Isaac signifies new hope, the future, birth according to the spirit of God and thus freedom.

Paul's use of this ancient story is a midrashic effort to show that the ancient story still has some value for Paul's readers. Both Isaac and

---

MIDRASH

A distinctive Jewish usage of the Old Testament, a meditation on the ancient text or an imaginative reconstruction of the scene to find contemporary applications. A precept may be retold (*halakhah*) or restated or an ancient episode (*haggadah*) may be retold—not their historical circumstances but in such a way as to give light and understanding to a new generation.

Ishmael were circumcised but this has nothing to do with the future hope for Isaac. Isaac takes his place as rightful heir because he was the child of promise. Circumcision had nothing to do with it. The Galatians are "like Isaac . . . children of promise" (4:28).

In the closing verses of this chapter Paul returns to his earlier theme of being born of the Spirit. Just as Isaac was a child of the Spirit of God so also are the Galatians. As the scriptures present Isaac as the chosen one, so the Galatians should accept their destiny as God's chosen apart from any demand of Jewish law. They are, in Paul's eyes, children of the free woman, released from all demands of law (4:31).

STUDY QUESTIONS

1. Does the Spirit come as a result of faith or law or good works or all of the above, or some of the above?

2. What do spirit and flesh mean?

3. God gives the Spirit and salvation as a gift, not as a result of what people do or do not do. What are the implications of this for Christian spirituality?

4. Who are, in truth, God's people? Why does this question cause problems?

5. Americans are law-abiding. How would Paul's concept of law affect the American understanding of law, both civil and ecclesiastical?

6. Does all law always have value?

7. Humanity is already reconciled. Unity has been established with

God. How can these ideas help to understand human life today both within and without the church?

8. Freedom seems to disturb many people. Why?

9. People can now call God "Abba." Why are many people still uncomfortable with God?

10. What ideas have appealed to you the most in these chapters of Galatians?

Chapter 8

FREEDOM, THE SPIRIT
AND THE CHRISTIAN LIFE

Suggested Scriptural Reading:

Galatians 5–6

Warning Against the Law (5:1–12)

This final section of Galatians (excluding the conclusion of the letter, 6:11–18) contains a series of warnings, some efforts to sum up Paul's position and some practical conclusions for living life in the Spirit. The concluding section is easier to divide from the rest (5:25–6:10) since it evidently was personally written by Paul himself. The verses from 5:1 to 6:10 comprise a mixture of doctrine and warnings. The central sentence is verse 1: "For freedom Christ has set us free; stand fast therefore and do not submit again to a yoke of slavery." In many ways this is the conclusion of the previous chapters and the introduction to what will follow.

Christ has already set us free and so a new set of imperatives confront humankind. Freedom has come from a divine choice in Christ. This has already taken place and now the Galatians are to participate in this freedom as the great gift of God. The individual who accepts this freedom does not retreat into self, seeking some kind of personal liberation. Rather the true searcher for freedom recognizes that freedom has been given from without. No longer need people discover freedom, but they must learn to accept it in loving obedience to God who has freed the person from law and sin and death. All this God has already accomplished on the Good Friday and Easter Sunday experience of Jesus.

Once a person has accepted this freedom it makes no sense to return to a previous slavery. Paul himself had once been part of the tradition of circumcision and law. It was of no use to him and will be of no use to the Galatians (5:2). Circumcision means nothing in light of the gospel of grace (5:2–4). To accept circumcision a Gentile has accepted the Torah, and this makes no sense in the light of the gospel of grace and freedom. Such strong words are unusual especially when one reads the seriousness of circumcision for Jews.

> This is my covenant which you shall keep between you and me and your descendants after you: every male among you shall be circumcised. You shall be circumcised in the flesh of your foreskins, and it shall be a sign of the covenant between me and you. He that is eight days old among you shall be circumcised; every male throughout your generations, whether born in your house or bought with your money from any foreigner who is not of your offspring, both he that is born in your house and he that is bought with your money, shall be circumcised. So shall my covenant be in your flesh an everlasting covenant. Any uncircumcised male who is not circumcised in the flesh of his foreskin shall be cut off from his people. He has broken my covenant (Gen 17:10–14).

For Paul, however, circumcision no longer makes any sense. In verses 5 and 6 Paul switches to the first person plural, contrasting the true Christian with the Galatians who are contemplating retreating into law and circumcision. Those who accept Christ in faith live in hope for the future, for they have received the Spirit and await full righteousness (5:5), acknowledging that circumcision or not makes no difference when you are dealing with the powerful love of God accepted in faith through Christ (5:6).

Some might wonder whether, when Paul concludes this long section with the words "faith working through love" (5:6), he is returning to a notion that love is the prerequisite for justification. No such thing is implied. Love is rather the expression of the faith. Christians are already loved by God and have already accepted this love in their faith. Now they are to become loving. The love they have received reaches out to embrace others.

The Galatians had been running well (5:7) and they should return to their previous course. They have been tempted to take another path, but this is not from God (5:8) but from without God.

Paul returns to an accusation leveled against him, and he himself then levels an accusation. We are not completely in the light about these verses (5:8–12) since we are left in the dark with regard to the accuser and the actual accusation. No doubt, however, exists in Paul's mind. With a certain sense of pique he suggests that those who advocate circumcision go all the way and castrate themselves (5:12). Paul once advocated circumcision but no longer (5:11). He preaches instead "the stumbling block of the cross" (5:11). That alone makes sense to him, and no other means of salvation exists. The very means of Christ's death, a scandal to the Jews who expected a powerful messiah, symbolizes new power. The event which seems to be a failure has become the means of salvation for Jew and Gentile. Circumcision was the sign of Jewish exclusivity; the cross, a scandal for Jew, has become the sign of inclusivity. How could anyone want to return to circumcision and the law after they have experienced the freedom of God's grace in Christ!

Spirit and Flesh (5:13–26)

Throughout this final section Paul chooses no fewer than fifteen imperatives, for he wishes his readers to exercise their freedom. He offers some general guidelines and some specific commands to give the Galatians a sense of how they can live this new freedom responsibly. Often people have emphasized the ethics in this final section as if it were devoid of all theology. Such is not the case. Paul intertwines his theology with the ethical exhortations.

Freedom does not mean an opportunity to live according to the flesh but to live for the sake of others (5:13). People have a choice to live in freedom for self or for others. Paul exhorts the living for others and gives the reason: loving fulfills the whole law (5:14). Almost immediately Paul turns his attention to the practical situation at Galatia which must have been filled with bickering and backbiting as a result of the controversy over circumcision and the law. "Stop it," says Paul (5:15).

Verse 16 again changes the scene and needs a more careful translation. The two verbs are not parallel imperatives—"walk by the Spirit . . . do not gratify the flesh"—but rather the second depends on the first. "Walk by the Spirit and then you will not gratify the desires of the flesh." Spirit and flesh, for Paul, live in contradiction (5:17); they make war on each other. This is reminiscent for the modern reader of what Paul will write in Romans (7:15–20). What a per-

---

IMPERATIVES OR IMPLIED IMPERATIVES

- stand fast (5:1)
- do not submit again to the yoke of slavery (5:1)
- do not use your freedom as an opportunity for the flesh (5:13)
- be servants of one another (5:13)
- take heed that you are not consumed by one another (if you devour each other) (5:15)
- walk by the Spirit (5:25)
- have no self-conceit, no provoking of one another, no envy (5:25)
- bear one another's burdens (6:2)
- let each one test his own work (6:4)
- share all good things (6:6)
- do not be deceived (6:7)
- do not grow weary in well-doing (6:9)
- do good to all, especially those in the household of the faith (6:10)

---

son wills the person often does not do, and what a person does not will that a person often will do. (A more complete explanation will be found when we treat this passage in Romans.) Spirit and flesh are in conflict, and the true believers follow the Spirit which will then release them from the law (5:18). The law has been like a dictator but the Spirit liberates and helps the individual deal with the problem of the flesh. Law never helped anyway. Now the Spirit helps and offers freedom.

Paul concludes with a list of what it means to live by the flesh (5:19–20) and what it means to live by the Spirit (5:21–22). The former brings all kinds of immorality; the latter brings peace and joy and patience and kindness and faithfulness and overcomes all the efforts of the flesh to pull down and destroy. The Spirit leads to these things and not the law. Those who have the Spirit have already dealt with the flesh (5:24) and live now according to the Spirit and so there exists with those people no self-deceit and no jealousy (5:26).

In many ways the second list provided here by Paul gives indications of the presence of the Spirit in a person's life. Life in community never is without its problems, but the Spirit brings these qualities which can make such a life a joy. Where the Spirit exists, people live patiently, and faithfully. They are gentle with each other and com-

Flesh	Spirit
immorality	love
impurity	joy
licentiousness	peace
idolatry	patience
sorcery	kindness
enmity	goodness
strife	faithfulness
jealousy	gentleness
anger	self-control
selfishness	no law
dissension	
party spirit	
envy	
drunkenness	
carousing	

passionate. Where instead jealousy and strife and hostility reign, the Spirit is surely not present.

The Fruits of the Spirit (6:1–10)

Those who are filled with the Spirit in freedom live according to the Spirit. They bear each other's burdens (6:1–5), encourage teachers (6:6), and persevere in good works (6:7–10). Often a believer needs help (6:1). They need to be restored "gently" with an awareness of one's own weakness. Burdens which are shared are more easily born (6:2); each one must bear the fair share (6:5), always with a look to avoiding self-satisfaction and complacency. Such will only produce a sense of superiority and arrogance which can never be a result of the Spirit.

In a community when one depends on another, pay close attention to those who teach the word and offer to them what they need (6:6). Often enough as Paul himself would know by experience, those committed to the word are overlooked and they too need support from the community.

Paul concludes with a look to the future and the results of what is happening now (6:7–9). The flesh leads to death; the Spirit leads to life. God knows the difference and God will not be mocked (6:7). While we live, we can always live according to who we are and what we have become because of the grace of God. Weariness may set in but can never rob the true believer of destiny. Remaining faithful in doing good brings its ultimate reward of life (6:9). While we live we always have the opportunity to do good especially to those of the household of God, the saints, the believers, those who have put aside the flesh and the law and have embraced the freedom of the Spirit through faith in Christ Jesus.

Paul does not conclude with a call to good works for salvation or justification but rather with a call to live in life what Christians have become. Those filled with the Spirit do not need a law to tell them to be kind to each other. Their faith in God directs them to live a life of faith and so they are kind to each other. They do not need a law to overcome the desires of the flesh; the Spirit already has overcome these powers and so they need only to live the life of the Spirit in faith. The conclusion is that eternal life naturally flows from the life of obedience to faith and not to a sense of personal justification through the performance or non-performance of works.

The Postscript (6:11–18)

And so the letter ends. Paul takes up the pen and adds in his own hand his final words. He sums up what he has tried to say. Quickly he mentions circumcision, flesh, law, the cross of Christ, boasting and persecution. He again attacks the motivation of his opponents (6:12–13) and reaffirms his commitment to the cross of Christ alone and not circumcision, for it means nothing (6:14–15). Finally he offers a blessing: Peace and mercy be upon all who "walk by this rule, upon the Israel of God" (6:16). The true Israel of God is those who walk according to the cross of Christ, accepting in faith the love of a gracious God who has reconciled humankind, Jew and Gentile alike as gift.

Paul himself has suffered and so can join in the suffering of Christ (6:17). He closes with a familiar blessing: "The grace of the Lord Jesus Christ be with your spirit" (6:18) which in fact is what he has been hoping and wishing and teaching the Galatians since he first began his letter to his erring community. He will not abandon them but lives in hope that he will be able to give thanks to God for all they have been. Unfortunately, we do not know how the letter to the Galatians was received. We have only Romans in which we detect a change in tone in Paul. The ultimate warrior for faith in the cross of Christ alone, he has battled for his cause. He will continue when he writes to the Romans.

STUDY QUESTIONS

1. Christians should live in freedom. What can this mean today? What are the obstacles to freedom? What is lacking in freedom?

2. Love is not the prerequisite for faith but the expression of faith. How does this affect the understanding of God and salvation?

3. Living by the Spirit helps. How can this be expressed in community and in an individual's spiritual life?

4. What do you like most about Galatians? Is the teaching helpful today? What do you dislike? Why? Why do many Christians seem to overlook Galatians?

5. How do good works fit in a gospel of freedom?

6. What are your thoughts on the relationship between Christians and Jews?

7. What imperatives from Paul do you like? Which do you dislike? Do imperatives help or hinder. Would Paul and his gospel be accepted today by most Christians?

SECTION III

The Epistle to the Romans

Chapter 9

INTRODUCTION TO ROMANS

History does makes fools of us all. Often what is spoken or written in haste or with anger or when even agitated does not reflect the true thought of the writer. Or, even more noteworthy, history can help us to change our minds.

The Paul of Galatians writes strongly, asserting that in no way can works bring about righteousness in the eyes of God. The Jewish law means nothing and contributes nothing to salvation. God gives freely the gift of salvation to Jew and Gentile alike. The emotional Paul wrote with fire in his words to a community he had converted and to whom he had given much of his life's energy.

Some like to think of Romans as more balanced or more reflective or more complete or even more nuanced. The sober Paul has refined his arguments and has written a theological treatise for the Roman church and for the church of all ages. Another possibility also exists to explain the change.

Paul probably lost his argument in his challenge at Antioch. He also may have lost in the reaction to the letter to the Galatians. Maybe he wrote too heatedly or with too much power or with not enough persuasion. And so when he came to write Romans he was willing to compromise a little. The observance of some Jewish practices for Jewish or even Gentile Christians would be acceptable provided no one believed they were necessary for salvation or justification. Paul changed his mind. He wanted to be part of a more general Christianity both to placate those Jewish Christians who wanted to maintain some of their Jewish historical roots in observance and to control some Gentile Christians who wanted to go too far in a law-free gospel. Romans presents a different and even a more tolerant Paul.

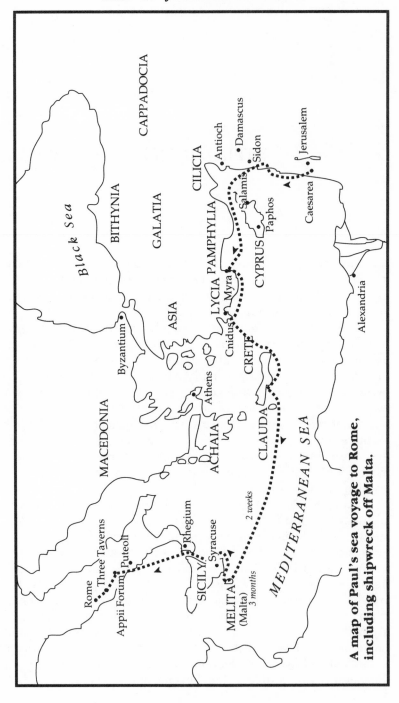

A map of Paul's sea voyage to Rome, including shipwreck off Malta.

> Since the Jews constantly made disturbances at the instigation
> of Chrestos, he [Claudius] expelled them from Rome
> (Suetonius, 25.4).

Roman Christianity

If Paul wrote Romans toward the end of the 50s and he had
wanted to go to Rome for some time (Rom 15:23), and if Suetonius
the Roman historian writes of Jews being expelled in 49 because of
some controversy over "Chrestos," then we know that Christianity
was in Rome in the 40s.

We also have a tradition that Rome was evangelized from Jerusalem, and most scholars will accept the position that a number of these
Jewish Christians were Judaizers, those wanting to maintain some of
the Jewish observances (moderate Judaizer) and those who claimed
that one first had to become a Jew before becoming a Christian (extreme Judaizer). Since Paul writes to the Christian community in
Rome with the mention of many names (16:3–16), we can also conclude that just as there were many synagogues in Rome, so there were
many or at least several house churches in Rome.

The presence of encouraging words to the strong and speaking of
the needs of the weak in chapter 14 also insinuates that the Roman
Christian community was divided. Inscriptions from the period show
that they were united in the same language (Greek) and may have
been predominantly Gentile but with strong Jewish influences. We
probably can conclude that Rome had several distinct groups which
can be discovered in Romans:

1. Jews who maintained their commitment to Judaism and
   rejected Christ and Christianity.

2. Jewish Christians who accepted Christianity but maintained
   some Jewish observances.

3. Jewish Christians who accepted Christianity and demanded
   that Gentiles first become Jews.

4. Gentiles who accepted Jewish observance (moderately or in
   an extreme way).

5. Gentiles who accepted a law-free gospel.

With such a variety of opinions the Christian community at Rome was divided, and Paul seems to have been aware of all of this. Even the question of the collection in chapter 15 would have caused a mixed reaction. The Jewish Christians loyal to Jerusalem may have been reluctant to involve themselves with a collection that was coming from law-free gospel communities. The Gentile Christians in Rome may have been reluctant to contribute to a Jerusalem church to avoid the idea that they were vassals and dependent upon their particular understanding of the Jesus tradition.

We also should note that at this period a strong nationalism existed among Jews and they would have been sensitive to anything that would violate Jewish distinctiveness and privileges. Thus for some Jews to preach that Gentiles could experience the same saving presence of God as Jews and without the law could easily cause conflict. This might explain the expulsion of Jews from Rome referred to by Suetonius. Those who advocated the acceptance of Gentiles without the observance of the law (followers of Paul) would have caused great tumult, especially since Christianity had not yet been separated from Judaism.

Paul's Situation in Writing Romans

No doubt Paul's gospel was suspect in Rome. No doubt that some of his converts were too liberal in their interpretation of the law-free gospel as evident in the problems in Corinth. His harsh words in Galatians probably reached Jerusalem and then might very well have reached the Christian communities in Rome as well.

Paul needed the Roman church to help him in the collection but also to use their influence with the Jerusalem church as a predominantly Gentile community with strong roots in Jerusalem. He needed to be accepted by both because he believed that the overriding necessity was the unity of the gospel and the unity of the church. Paul did not want to advocate two separate churches and so was willing to compromise to bring about a sense of unity between the Jewish Christians and the Gentile Christians. He wanted to promote mutual tolerance and esteem within the community, and his letter and his journey were directed to that end. This also would give him a good base as he pushed on to Spain and continued to preach his gospel to the Gentiles.

Paul had changed his approach but not his fundamental teaching.

OUTLINE OF ROMANS

I. Introduction 1:1–17

II. The Gospel of Jesus 1:18–8:39
   Universal Sin 1:18–3:20
   The Gospel of Faith 3:21–4:25
   Reconciliation, Salvation and Faith 5:1–8:39

III. Israel, Christianity and God's Grace 9–11

IV. The Living of Graced Believers 12:1–15:13

V. Conclusion 15:14–33

VI. Greetings to Romans 16:1–23

VII. Thanksgiving 16:25–27

In Galatians he preached a justification by faith apart from the law. In Romans he preached the righteousness of God revealed through faith apart from the law to the Jews and then to the Gentiles. His one gospel is universal even if he admitted that for the sake of peace and unity, if some Jewish Christians wanted to observe some Jewish practices, that was acceptable provided that they were not imposed on Gentiles. For their part, the Gentiles should respect these historical Jewish roots and continue to have esteem for the fellow Christians of Jewish origin even if they chose to observe some Jewish practices. In this way he could encourage the strong but also maintain a support for the weak. Unity remained his chief concern.

Reasons for Romans

The debate about the reason or reasons for Romans continues. The best answer seems to be that Paul had many reasons.

1. He considered himself the apostle to the Gentiles, and since Rome was a predominantly Gentile church he had apostolic responsibility for them.

2. He wanted all Christians in Rome to recognize that God offered universal salvation apart from the law.

3. He wanted to defend his gospel as authentic and was not ashamed of it.

4. He needed the support of the Roman church in his mission to Jerusalem.

5. He had specific problems in mind when he wrote, e.g. the observance or non-observance of Jewish holidays and the question of eating meat and drinking wine.

6. He wanted mutual tolerance and esteem among the various members of the Roman church and saw his mission to implant this.

Above all, Paul is a messenger in the service of the same gospel which Christians acknowledge all over the empire. This one preaching invited Jew and Gentile alike to accept the gracious love of God offered to all apart from the law, through his Son Jesus the Christ (Rom 1:2–4).

STUDY QUESTIONS

1. Does compromise and seeking balance help in life? What are the positive elements involved and the negative elements?

2. Paul seems to have lost his argument in Galatians and has rethought his position in Romans. Does this fit his personality?

3. Roman Christianity was conservative. What value does this approach offer?

4. Unity is worth working for, and so Paul compromises. What implications can be drawn from this change in positions for the contemporary church?

Chapter 10

UNIVERSAL SIN

Suggested Scriptural Reading:

Romans 1–3:30

Opening Greeting (1:1–17)

The opening greeting of Romans in some ways follows the traditional opening of a letter both for Paul and for his contemporaries. He identifies himself (1:1) and greets his recipients; "To all God's beloved in Rome who are called to be saints" (1:7). The greeting differs, however, from all of his other letters by its length and by the content.

Certainly Paul was writing in unusual circumstances. He did not found this community, nor had he visited it previously. Moreover, we have already noted that Paul and his preaching was of considerable controversy in this community. He did not know how he would be received whether personally or through his correspondence. He also needed this community and wanted to lay claim to his responsibility for all Gentile churches. In such a situation all care would be needed in how he began his letter to avoid a bad impression. Since Paul was probably known to many at Rome only by his reputation, he would have to set out his credentials more carefully. All of these factors contributed to his lengthy introduction.

He begins by asserting his apostleship, as one called by God, and then quotes what must have been a traditional formula, probably known to the Romans. If this non-Pauline formula was known to the Romans, then Paul was asserting that he was indeed a servant of the same Lord whom the Christians in Rome already acknowledged and loved.

The gospel concerning his Son who was descended from David according to the flesh and designated Son of God in power according to the Spirit of holiness by his resurrection from the dead, Jesus Christ our Lord (1:3–4).

The formula itself is a little unusual. It asserts that Jesus was descended from David, and thus Jewish, which would have suited this particular audience which had Jewish roots, and then the formula uses an unusual expression which hints at adoptionism: "designated Son of God in power through the Spirit of holiness by his resurrection . . ." (1:4). The "in power" (which some think was an addition either by Paul or by someone before him to avoid adoptionism) implies that the messiah became capable of being the messiah for others because of the spirit of holiness possessed by Jesus before the resurrection. The resurrection culminates who he was. At the very least, it is a lower christology than what is typical of Paul but one probably recognized by the Roman community.

Within this exposition of material that would have been familiar to the Romans he slips in not only his call to apostleship but also his responsibility for "all the nations" (1:5). Paul is *their* apostle too! Moreover since he greets "all" in Rome (1:7) he writes not just to those who are his supporters but to everyone, both the strong and the weak, in the churches at Rome (chapters 14–15). He not only wants to be accepted in Rome but wishes the Romans to live as one community of faith. Even his greeting of "grace and peace" are more than just some traditional Christian greetings. God's grace freely offered will be a dominant theme of Romans, and peace is needed not only within the Roman community but also between Paul and this community.

After this initial greeting, with its carefully orchestrated claim to an authentic gospel, Paul continues his efforts to make himself acceptable to this community (1:8–15). He attests that their faith is well known and he himself not only prays for them but has desired to come to them.

In verse 11 he continues his claim to apostleship among them by offering a spiritual gift but then quickly modifies this verse by tactfully referring to being "mutually encouraged by each other's faith (1:12). In 13 and 14 he returns to this claim to being an apostle for the Romans just as he is meant to preach to all Gentiles, to Greeks and barbarians.

Verses 16 and 17 present briefly his gospel which in turn will launch him into a detailed development, precisely for the Romans, in the body of the letter. Paul begins boldly by stating that he is not ashamed of his gospel. No doubt some in Rome thought that Paul should be ashamed, for it was a law-free gospel which might even be interpreted that God had abandoned his promise to Israel and had forsaken his convenantal commandments in the law. If Paul had proclaimed in Galatians that righteousness is God's gift apart from works, here he proclaims that God himself is righteous, offering salvation to all, Jew and Gentile, through faith. The rest of this letter up to chapter 12 will be Paul's defense that:

1. God remains righteous and faithful.
2. God offers salvation to all, Jew and Gentile.
3. Faith is the appropriate human response.

Paul in this letter focuses on the character of God as righteous in spite of salvation offered to all. Such a universal saving activity resulted from God's righteousness, and finally the results of this righteous activity brought righteousness in human life and in the world. God had set things right for humankind and creation. All three had to be included in his defense:

1. Paul's ministry in fact did promote human righteousness.

2. The God who promoted this conduct according to Paul was in fact righteous (although this affected a change in the understanding of the promise to Israel and the convenantal law).

3. Both the activity by Paul and others who followed this gospel and the putting aside of the law and expanding the promises made to Israel truly demonstrated that God remained righteous.

Sin and a False God (1:18–23)

The very choice of a division of this section is under question. Some commentators consider the first seventeen verses as the introductory material to the letter and begin with verse 18 with an examination of the citation of humanity under sin. A more careful reading of the verses, however, shows a close connection between verses 17 and 18, and, for that matter, a connection that works backward to verse 14. For this reason Achtemeier makes his division 1:14–3:20 and titles it "The Gospel and God's Wrath."

The problem seems to lie in dividing a letter which was never meant to be divided. The traditional division into chapter and verse often enough hinders the reader as much as helps. Whether or not

Paul begins the body of his letter with 14 or 17 or 18, we know that verse 17 announces his basic theme and that by verse 18 Paul has launched his first part of his carefully constructed argument: universal sin.

The wrath of God, the opposite of the righteousness of God, has been revealed against all who have substituted a false god in place of the true God. Creation reveals the creator, and all creatures are able to discern that presence. The root of all sin is the human tendency to substitute a false god for the one true God, whether that false god be expressed in terms of images of animals or mortals. People may claim to be wise, but in fact they are foolish, for instead of choosing immortality they choose mortality, and instead of following the wisdom of the creator they turn to the creature.

Sin in Control (1:24–32)

Instead of writing about catastrophes that will befall anyone who turns from the one true God, Paul merely remarks that the wrath of God directs humanity to turn to itself. Sin takes control of people and they suffer the consequences. God need not intervene, for sin itself is its own punishment. The abuse of the created order brings about the abuse of creatures and, for Paul in particular, the abuse of people and their sexuality. For Paul, when people just do whatever they want, then they have violated the sacred trust in nature. In this section we should not look upon the list of sins as exhaustive. They illustrate what happens when people have exchanged their birthright as God's creation for an idolatry which ignores the one true God and substitutes another. Any type of improper conduct destroys the peace and unity that should characterize God's created human society. Paul's references to homosexuality or lesbianism should not be understood as a condemnation of homosexuals or lesbians. The culture of Paul's day involved homosexual practices which were often associated with worship and with a type of practiced sexuality which included a general depravity. This is not the same understanding that we have today of people who have a relatively exclusive gender orientation. Homosexuality or lesbianism, however, can be destructive of human society just as can envy, strife, conceit, gossip, and haughty people (1:29–30). Paul picks out some examples of sin which can be destructive of humans as examples of what happens when people give up the true God and follow a false god. Paul does not write to condemn but rather asks people to repent and accept the righteousness of God which God freely offers.

Verse 32 may seem a little strange. What Paul notes is that people who commit such sins also encourage others to do likewise. Humans seem to have the tendency to try to make private sin public policy and acceptable. Such tendencies continue today with the practice of allowing private greed to become public policy and acceptable almost with immunity.

The Power of Sin (2:1–16)

To continue to do evil brings God's wrath even if one attempts to maintain an appearance of doing what is right. No one should feel superior to another since all are under the same power of sin. God may very well let evil go unpunished, but that is not to lead people to believe that evil has no consequences but rather that people might be tempted to repent. The kindness of God in not destroying evil people must not be presumed but rather should lead the person to disclaim that evil and turn to God and seek forgiveness (2:4–5). The day of judgment will come when God will give eternal life and glory and honor and peace to those who have done good, and wrath and fury to those who obey wickedness. No difference will be made for Jew or Greek, for all are to be judged equally.

Gentiles who by birth (by nature) do not have the law can still do good, just as the Jews who know the law can do good. Since God is the one creator of all, God will be impartial in his goodness and in judgment. People can learn enough about God at least to the extent that people are God's creatures (1:19–20) and thus they are able to act responsibly before that same God (2:14–15) whether they have the law or not. The argument seems clear: both Jews and Gentiles have sinned and both Jews and Gentiles can know enough about God to do what is right. A universal God has created all people and has allowed all people to live under the power of sin and allows all people the possibility of turning from sin and accept forgiveness and grace.

Sin and God's People (2:17–29)

Although writing to an audience which has Jewish Christians and even Gentile Christians strongly affected by Jewish traditions, Paul startles his audience with his critique of the "upright" Jew. Previously Paul had included the Jew in his universal condemnation of sin, but now in this section he turns specifically to the Jewish people, for they have had a special relationship to God in the past.

All have sinned, Jew and Gentile.

All can know something of God.

All are God's creatures.

All people live under the power of sin.

All can accept forgiveness and grace.

One might assume that as chosen people the Jews are exempt from the wrath of God. After acknowledging what Jews might be in relationship to others—guide, light, corrector, teacher (2:19–20)—Paul accuses them of doing precisely what they have condemned in others. It makes no difference belonging to the chosen people if one does the same as everyone else. The law will not protect the guilty. Chosenness, law and circumcision mean nothing if people do not live responsibly. In fact such chosen people bring dishonor upon the God whom they pretend to serve (2:24). The real Jewishness is something internal and not external (2:28). Paul is quick to acknowledge that many of the virtues associated with the law can be practiced as well by people who are not under the law. The Jews cannot claim exclusiveness by their law, since Gentiles can also actually do the same things as Jews even though they are ignorant of the law. Neither ignorance (Gentile) nor knowledge (Jews) can protect people from the coming wrath of God. God will judge impartially (2:6).

The Evil That People Do (3:1–8)

And so what value is found in being a Jew? If Jewishness and circumcision are primarily internal, then what value can be found in the external circumcision and the identification with the Jewish people? Paul raised the question, and to it he must respond.

After what he has written on the universality of wrath, one might expect Paul to say that being a Jew and being circumcised have no value. On the contrary, for him they have much value. To the Jews belong the oracles (convenantal promises) of God, and in spite of all unfaithfulness God remains faithful. Some might wonder if then we could conclude that since the placing of God's faithfulness in such a prominent light results in goodness, might this then excuse the presence of evil? Paul says by no means (*me genoito;* this unusually strong Greek expression will be used often in this letter and signifies: in no way, by no means, of course not, don't be silly, etc.). The evil is still evil. Perhaps some people accused Paul of condoning evil to make the faithfulness of God more evident. Paul rejects such an interpretation. We cannot do evil even if good will follow and people are still responsible for the evil they do (3:8).

No One Is Righteous (3:9–20)

The conclusion is evident—universal sin: "None is righteous, no not one" (3:10). Humanity has rebelled against its creator (3:10–18) and even the law will not protect the Jews (3:19–20). Wrath and sin abound which will set the scene for Paul to begin to write of God's grace.

Paul completes his indictment against the law and the Jews by turning to the scriptures themselves, and he compiles a collection principally from the psalms (Pss 14:1–2; 53:1–2; 5:9; 140:3; 10:7; 3:15–17; 36:1; Is 59:7–8). Such a compilation wipes out any claim to righteousness. No one can lay claim to being free from sin and thus unworthy of the wrath of God. The works of the law will not justify (3:20) and the whole world stands accountable before God (3:19). Sin is universal. Sin finds its place under the law and even in piety. The grace of God can alone make a difference.

STUDY QUESTIONS

1. All have sinned. How is this evident in the world today?

2. God alone saves. What images of God do you have? Have these images been affected by the study of Paul, especially in Romans?

3. If sin is no longer in control, then why is there so much evil in the world?

4. Is the great sin really to think that people can merit salvation on their own by good works?

5. Why does Paul criticize the upright Jew?

6. Do you really think that all people are worthy of the wrath of God?

Chapter 11

THE GOSPEL OF FAITH

Suggested Scriptural Reading:

Romans 3:21–8:39

Christ and Faith (3:21–31)

And where is human hope? If the past is the past of sin and rebellion and disobedience, whether of Jew or Gentile, if all deserve the wrath of God, then what future can humankind believe in? The past has brought rebellion against God by making false gods and even by attempting to make gods of each other. No one has escaped and no one has privilege, even those who are called the chosen of God. After reading the first section of the body of this letter, people might feel little more than despair. But Paul changes his tone: the righteousness of God has been revealed through faith in Jesus Christ for all who believe (3:22). Jesus can restore the broken fabric of humanity by restoring humanity's relationship to God. Through Jesus, God demonstrates his righteousness and offers us the hope of receiving righteousness. Since all have sinned, both Jew and Gentile, God has justified humanity as gift. Humanity's unrighteousness by sin has brought about the abandonment by God of humanity, and so people have been left to their own devices. But now God wishes to restore a good relationship with humanity which is God's righteousness by grace in Jesus. Paul began this theme in 1:16–17 but then followed his gospel with the section on the power of evil and sin. Now he returns with his gospel of hope for all, with no distinction (3:22) between Jew and Gentile. People cannot create divinity for themselves but must give up all reliance on their own efforts to establish their relationship with

96

The righteousness of God is revealed in Jesus.

Faith in Jesus restores humanity's relationship with God.

God has justified all as gift.

God. God alone will restore what is lost, and he will do so by Christ when people accept Christ in faith.

Verses 25 and 26 show that the death of Christ on the cross is the sign of the righteousness of God, and by faith in Christ God makes it possible for all to become righteous. By sending his Son and allowing his Son to die on the cross, God demonstrates his faithfulness to a sinful creation. The no of sinful humanity to the goodness of Jesus, in the words of Karl Barth, becomes the yes of God to righteousness. Moreover, if people will trust in Jesus rather than in themselves or anything they might do, they also can be reconciled and restored in their relationship to God. If people no longer have to prove themselves worthy of love but can count on a loving God, then humanity in turn can deal with itself in restoring loving relationships among all peoples.

Both Jew and Gentile now fall under the judgment of faith and not by any observance. Works of humanity can never allow the individual to stand in the presence of God with dignity. Only God's gracious gift makes such a position possible. The one God of both Jew and Gentile justifies both on the basis of faith and not law.

Again, one might conclude that faith and law are opposing elements and that now the law has been overthrown by faith. We must remember Paul's audience. He will not just throw out the traditions so dear to many of his listeners. He wishes to lead them to a better understanding of the meaning of the law, and so in verse 31 he comes to an unexpected conclusion: the law is not overthrown but it is actually upheld! Paul will explain the true basis for the law and so he will turn to Abraham.

Abraham, Father in Faith (4:1–25)

Abraham the father of Israel continues to hold a primary position in Judaism, and, as far as Paul is concerned, also in Christianity. God once asked him to give up his past and travel from Ur of the Chaldeans to Canaan (Gen 11:31). Abraham responded in faith and moved from his homeland. Later he would be asked to give up his future in the sacrifice of his son Isaac (Gen 22:1–18). Abraham was judged righteous in the sight of God because of his faith in God. Paul had written of Abraham in Galatians. He returns to his model in Romans.

Paul is interested in Abraham in this chapter for two reasons:

1. Abraham was justified not because of anything he did, for God has so declared him just both before circumcision and thus also before the law (Gen 15:6).
2. Abraham is the bearer of promised blessings for all peoples (Gen 12:2–3).

If Abraham was justified by what he had done, he would have reason to boast (4:2), but because Abraham received justification apart from any works, then he received it through faith as a gift (4:4–5). Abraham becomes the perfect example of the kind of faith that Paul will use in explaining the gift of grace through faith in Jesus Christ.

Faith and Law

What is also significant in the mind of Paul is the relationship between faith and the law. Recall that he does not wish to destroy Jewish roots and in particular wants to be sensitive to the feelings of the Jewish Christian community at Rome. He will not attempt to have faith supersede the law but rather will place the law in its proper perspective. The faith of Abraham preceded the law, and the law in turn must rest upon faith. Abraham then becomes the key to interpreting the law and its meaning not only for himself but for all future generations. Law does not justify but only faith. Faith will always precede law and the law will take an inferior position to faith.

Paul continues his argument by appealing to Psalm 32:1–2 in which the supposed author David also presents the belief that God declares righteousness apart from any works (4:6–8). Slowly Paul encourages his Jewish audience to consider that his teaching is not contrary to the Jewish traditions but rather flows from these traditions. Who better than Abraham could Paul use to present his case?

Abraham, Father of All

Since Paul also was dealing with the question of Gentiles, Abraham also gives him an opportunity to broaden those included. Circumcision, one of the principal distinguishing aspects of Judaism both in the Gentile world and in the mind of Paul, has nothing to do with righteousness. If Abraham was declared justified before circumcision, then righteousness is for both the circumcised and the uncircumcised (4:9–11). Abraham can be the father of those who are circumcised since he accepted this sign of his relationship to God (4:12). He can also be the father of those who are not circumcised since he was declared righteous apart from circumcision (4:11). By so weaving his argument, Paul has set the possibility of acceptance of the Gentiles by the Jews and the Jews by the Gentiles within the Roman Christian community. Abraham, the father of Judaism and the one destined to bless all nations, easily fulfills Paul's set purpose.

Abraham is the father of both circumcised and uncircumcised because of his faith (4:13). The law could not bring the fulfillment of God's promises since no one could observe the law completely, and in fact the law was transgressed and brought sin and wrath (4:15). The promise to Abraham came as God's gracious gift and not as any demand of the observance of any law. Only if sin has no chance of breaking the relationship to God can the promises ever be fulfilled. Such is possible not through law but through faith (4:16–18). Faith upheld Abraham. He would become the father of many nations (4:17) not because of anything he or his descendants did but because God would remain faithful to his promise. Even when he saw little hope for a future because of his old age, Abraham still trusted in God's promise (4:19–20) and did not waver because he believed that God could do all things, that God could fulfill his promises (4:21).

In verse 23 Paul begins his transition. He has led his readers to see the close relationship to Christian faith and the faith of Abraham for all, Jew and Gentile. Now he can turn to his understanding of justification through faith in Jesus Christ. The foundation has been laid in Old Testament traditions, bringing this tradition up to the present for Paul (4:23). For as Abraham was declared just, so the same will be true for Paul's communities, whether of Jewish origin or Gentile origin, on the basis of their faith in him who raised Jesus from the dead (4:24). Finally Paul has set the stage to deal with righteousness now for all who believe in the Jesus who has died for sins (4:25a) and who rose for humankind's justification (4:25b).

Reconciliation (5:1–11)

Evil and sin brought Jesus to the cross, but the power of goodness and the faithfulness of God brought Jesus to life in his resurrection. As a result, humankind can now be at peace with God (5:1). Sin will not destroy the relationship with God because God has so declared.

These first five verses are similar to other almost ecstatic outbursts by Paul. He has made his declaration of faith in the God who raised Jesus. Now Paul exults in the effects for humankind that had been delivered not only from sin and evil but also from the burden of attempting to maintain a relationship with God through appropriate works. Humanity can have hope for the future (5:2), for now people can stand in the presence of God as justified, reconciled, holding the possibility of sharing the glory, the goodness and the power of God. This assured hope can bring a confidence that will withstand any opposition. Sufferings mean nothing. The person of faith can endure all things which in turn only strengthens the hope (5:3–4). No one can ever be disappointed in God. Already those who believe and hope have experienced the outpouring of the Spirit giving people a taste of the love of God which overcomes all difficulties (5:5). All this has become possible because Christ died for humanity when all were sinners (5:6). How very strange that God would show such love through Christ to overcome evil and sin in a sinful humanity (5:7–8). And if God sent his Son to a sinful humanity and now this humanity has been declared justified through the blood of Christ (5:9), then humanity need never fear the wrath of God. If God could love a sinful humanity and restore a loving relationship, then humanity can only look forward to the saving presence of God in their lives (5:10). People are now reconciled, apart from circumcision, apart from the law, but only through the Lord Jesus Christ (5:11). How appropriate is rejoicing in the goodness of God to all humankind, both Jew and Gentile. For Paul, if all have been reconciled with God, then surely they can be reconciled with each other.

Adam, Christ and Original Sin (5:12–21)

For centuries this section was interpreted as the scriptural foundation for original sin. The theology of original sin from Augustine through the medieval discussions, through Trent and down to the present time, involves more of course than just what Paul presents here in Romans. Contemporary theologians will speak of original sin as being born into a sinful condition, ratifying this condition by sinful action and also experiencing a lack of true or proper relationship to God through grace. Although contemporary in their explanations, all of these elements are present in Paul and in this section.

Paul surely knows that humanity has sinned (5:12), for all humanity has ratified the sin of Adam (5:12a). All have fallen under the power of sin. The only chance of not being under the power of sin is to

---

Evil brought Jesus to the cross.

The goodness of God raised Jesus.

Humankind is now at peace with God.

Humanity is delivered from sin.

People can stand justified, reconciled.

Suffering now means nothing.

People have already received the Spirit.

People are reconciled apart from the law, circumcision or good works.

All, Jew and Gentile, should rejoice in the goodness of God.

---

have another possibility of being truly human and without sin. Such is possible through the new Adam. What Adam caused, Jesus undid. Adam had failed in his relationship to God and Jesus succeeded in not only maintaining his relationship with God but making it possible for all to be reconciled. Jesus did not ratify the sinful condition of humanity; Jesus lived a life of grace and thus overcame the curse of Adam's sin. Now humanity can be delivered from the power of the evil condition, can live a life of the justified and can experience the grace of God through faith.

The universal consequences of Adam's disobedience brought the universality of sin and death (5:12) apart from the law. People lived in this sinful environment even before Moses (5:14). All experienced the reality of sin and thus of death. This is not the place to discuss the possibility of immortal life apart from sin. Rather, Paul thinks of the evil that people face in dying and the contrast of sure hope that Christians have in the presence of death because of the hope of eternal life.

Power of Grace

The power to bring sin into the world differs from the power that brings life and justification (5:15–17). Grace is more powerful than

trespass of one → condemnation for all

righteousness of one → acquittal and life for all

disobedience of one → all sinners

obedience of one → righteousness for all

law, trespass, sin, death, → grace, righteousness, life

sin even if sin has ruled human history. People often may have the impression that sin has more than abounded. Such a viewpoint fails to see the power of grace which actually brings about a reconciliation between sinful humanity and God apart from anything that humanity may do. Surely grace is more powerful if grace accomplished reconciliation and justification. Paul can conclude this section with a declared parallel between Adam and Christ (5:18–19):

Christ sets humanity in a new direction, in a new relationship to God. The goal now is life and begins with an experience of justification and reconciliation. Humanity has been declared right in the eyes of God because of Christ. The long reign of sin always begetting sin has given way to a new age in which grace becomes the response to sin. The new father of the human race has overtaken the old father of the human race. Christ has become the second Adam. Where evil and sin abounded, now grace abounds.

Often enough Christians of every age have falsely concluded that if God's grace is more powerful than evil and sin, then evil and sin mean nothing and it matters little if we sin or do evil. God's grace will overcome all sin and evil. Paul responds to this false interpretation of grace in the following section.

Baptism, Sin and Grace (6:1–14)

Sin, grace and law are all interrelated in the mind of Paul. We can never understand the past nor appreciate the present and hope for the future unless we see how these human dimensions influence each other and how ultimately grace triumphs.

In this section Paul repeats the same Greek phrase (*to oun*, what then or what therefore) three times.

Each section begins with the same question, *to oun*, followed by a

to oun, shall we sin so that grace shall abound (v. 1)?

to oun, shall we sin because we are not under law but grace (v. 15)?

to oun, is the law sin (7:7)?

possible inference followed by a strong denial: *me genoita* (we have already seen this expression, meaning: by no means, no way!). His emphasis on grace and the goodness of God could lead to a misunderstanding on the part of some, and no doubt this was the situation as reported in Rome. Paul had raised these issues in chapters 4 and 5, and so he continues to deal with his teaching in chapters 6 and 7. The very presence of the formula attracts the reader or the listener to follow the argument contained in both chapters as part of one carefully developed thought by Paul. Each section builds on what precedes and culminates with a sure hope that God delivered Paul from this power of sin and death through Christ Jesus (7:25a).

After Paul has declared that "in no way" may we continue in sin so that grace shall abound, the reader might expect to find a long section on the power of evil and sin and the terrible temptation to test the goodness of God. Instead he merely says that anyone who has died to sin is delivered from sin (6:2). This thought brings Paul to his declaration on the meaning of baptism.

If people have already experienced a share in the death of the Lord, then they are already dead to sin precisely because they are dead (6:6). The dead can no longer rebel against God, and for Paul those who have been baptized in Christ are freed from the power of sin. Some of this thought may cause some confusion, but for Paul baptism really causes a participation in the death of Christ (6:3–4) and so that is over. Of course it does not help very much if we just remain dead, and so Paul states that having died in Christ we will rise with him (6:4–5). He makes it clear by his use of the past tense that we truly have died, but when referring to the resurrection he uses the future tense to signify that we are yet to fully experience this new life as resurrected (6:5b, 8b). While awaiting the fullness of that new life in the future, we live now a life in Christ which gives us the power not to sin. People need not sin and they will not sin if they respond to the life they have in Christ Jesus (6:10–11).

The results of this new life make the difference and Paul makes his first moral exhortation as a result of what people have become through faith. No longer are people condemned to rebel, to make false gods for themselves, to allow evil to control them (6:12–13). Sin has given way to grace and now people can respond by grace to a loving God who has made them righteous (6:13–14). Grace makes it possible for people to live a life freed from the compulsion to sin and the inevitability to sin.

The freedom given by baptism will not become completely evident until the fullness of this new age, but it has begun for Paul and makes it possible for people to overcome the sin that surrounds them. People's actions should portray who they are, and through baptism they are new creations, dead to sin with the promise of a new life that will be realized completely only in the future.

This passage also includes Paul's thought on baptism as the means by which this new reality begins. Baptism expresses the faith that in Christ Jesus, God has reconciled humankind, has overcome evil, sin and death. Reconciliation still depends upon faith, but for Paul this faith finds an external expression in a ritual of water washing. New relationships have opened up for humanity through faith in Christ, and this is expressed within the community in baptism.

Christ, the New Master (6:15–23)

The second section contrasts law and grace which also would have been significant for Paul's readers. We still can sin. No one has any trouble identifying with that! But people cannot just do what they wish. Paul used the analogy of a slave. In ancient society the master had complete dominion, and a slave totally submitted to the will of the master. In the past people had served the master of sin and now a new master had entered the picture, the Lord Jesus. People cannot serve both but must live a life based on following obediently the new master they have in Christ Jesus (6:16–18). The submission to the new master in Christ Jesus has brought a liberation from sin, law and death and people should live accordingly. Then they will live righteously instead of how they had lived previously (6:19).

To fortify his belief, Paul recalls for his readers their past. They might be tempted to rethink how they had lived, and if they do, they should remember what their previous way of living brought them— death (6:21). No one wants to die. Everyone wants to live forever, and so in this new way of living, Paul reminds them that they can look forward to eternal life (6:22–23). Surely the hope of eternal life

---

Marriage binds while the spouse lives.

At the death of a spouse, a new marriage is possible.

The law was the spouse.

Jesus has died and so people can have a new spouse.

The new spouse is the Spirit which frees from the law.

---

makes the former way of living unappealing. People often enough wanted to do the right thing, but the enslavement to sin made it impossible. Now activities and behavior can follow desires. With faith comes the power to respond and express faith in action.

Law (7:1–6)

Thus far Paul has not dealt with the question of law. He introduced the idea in the beginning of this section (6:15) but then went on to discuss sin and the effects of faith and grace. In 7:1–6 he returns to the thought of law. Being under grace and not under law does not give Christians the right to do whatever they please, to sin, and pay no attention to their actions. But by baptism Paul does believe that people are also freed from the law. Paul makes his response by using an example that seems rather confused. The marriage relationship binds one spouse while the other one lives (7:2). Upon death, what had been forbidden is now possible for the surviving partner (7:3). The analogy becomes clearer. Previously the law was the spouse, but the death of Christ has made it possible for the believer to take on a new partner. Here the analogy fails since it is the death of a third party, but the thought can still be understood: law is dead for the believer and now the believer has a new spouse (7:4). As a partner with a new spouse, the believer can live a life of the Spirit (7:6). These topics—sin, law and Spirit—Paul will develop further in the rest of the chapter and the following chapter. Life in the flesh, life under the power of sin, can lead only to death (7:5). Life according to the Spirit is the new life of obedience to God, separated from both sin and law (7:6).

Paul is not going to equate sin (7:7) with law but will affirm its goodness (7:12). In itself the law might be considered neutral, which makes it both strong and weak. The law can falsely encourage people to think that they can save themselves through its observance. But when people are freed from such false conceptions, then the law can give some guidance in how to live according to this new relationship with God and others. God had given the law, and so for Paul it cannot be evil, but people have such a propensity to think that they can erect their own actions to a level of demanding God to respond that they become idolators. The law is not evil but has been perverse in the history of humankind. Paul will continue this perspective as he examines law from the perspective of grace in the following section.

Grace Overcomes Law and Sin (7:7–25)

The fundamental question that persists in understanding this section of Romans is the identity of the "I." The second question for careful study is the relationship between the law and sin. Both are interrelated but can also be examined separately.

Sin Used the Law

For Paul the law results in evil acts. Also for him, sin is the controlling force which causes these evil acts. Sin had used the commandments to bring about evil results. Sin reversed the intent of the law by bringing death rather than life (7:9–10). The law itself is not evil but holy and just and good (7:12). The law can help us in how to live and can assist us in being obedient to God, but sin has perverted the law. Sin has caused people to think that they can depend upon themselves and upon personal moral achievements and thus can lay claim upon God. Sin, by using the law, caused people to rely on themselves rather than upon the mercy and goodness of God, and that is the greatest evil. Sin has taken the law which is good, sin has taken people created good, and perverted both. No longer is the law an expression of how to live but a tool used by sin to delude God's good creation. The law did not bring death to humankind, by no means (*me genoita*) (7:13), but sin used the law and in so doing the power of sin became evident as sin (7:13b). But now people need not continue to live under the power of sin through the power of Christ.

Who Is "I"

But who is the "I?" Some have interpreted the "I" in these verses as referring to Paul the Pharisee; others think it refers to Christians, others to Adam and others to humanity in general. We can begin by saying that it does not refer to Paul, neither the Pharisee nor the Christian. It cannot refer to Paul the Pharisee, since nowhere do we have any evidence that he ever thought of himself in despair in attempting to fulfill the law. Rather, he seems to think that he fulfilled the law beyond measure. Nor does it refer to Paul the Christian since he believes that all Christians are given the Spirit which enables them to live a life of grace.

The Power of Sin over Individuals

Often enough in the history of Christianity verses 14–25 have been interpreted to refer to general Christian existence. But if we place these verses in the context of baptism in chapter 6 and the Spirit in chapter 8, then these verses cannot refer to Christian existence. Believers have died to sin and are already freed from sin (6:7, 11, 17, 18, etc.). If the baptized Christian is dead to sin and freed from the law, then Paul cannot be referring to the Christian when he states: "But I am carnal, sold under sin" (7:14). The point of these verses seems rather to be the total power of sin over individuals. It does not deal with a moral imperative to try to do better but with a sense of the power of sin which is total. And so we still are left with the question: To whom do these verses refer?

Some have seen the passage as referring to Adam after he had sinned, but if so, since Adam stands for humanity, then these verses deal with humanity in general and not Paul and not the Christian. In that case they would have little relevance to believers.

Non-Christian Life Under the Law

The verses probably refer to Paul's vision of non-Christian life under the law but from his perspective of Christianity. Paul had known that the law was good. In fact the law expressed God's will and he himself attempted to live according to this law. He also thought himself successful, which was the problem or the sin. He began to think of himself as capable of controlling God and God's behavior by his own actions. He acted as if he could accomplish his own salvation. He could merit God's love by his own devices. He could discern and accomplish what God expected and then he could stand in God's presence and demand his reward. Such a position made him unable to relate to God as expressed in Christ Jesus. His devotion to the law led him to reject the final expression of God's will for humanity in Christ. He intended to do good but he did evil (7:21). Paul sees the law as useless for fulfilling the true will of God, for the true will of God is faith in the Lord Jesus alone. Apart from Christ humanity will continue to do evil even as it attempts to do good (7:22–23). Christ alone could destroy the power of sin over all humanity so that people can learn to serve the true God under grace, freed from sin and the law. The dilemma of humanity without Christ is that people try to serve God with their mind, with their intentions, but in ordinary human life (flesh) they serve sin, for they depend more on themselves than upon God. The only one who can deliver humanity from this strange dilemma of wanting to do good and wanting to trust in God and wanting to live in obedience to God is Christ (7:25). He offers the possibility of salvation and reconciliation not because of what a person has done but because of what God has done. Then this same person can live a life in Christ and the actions and behavior will follow.

This understanding of these verses might cause some discomfort for contemporary believers since no longer can they just identify themselves with these verses. No longer can believers feel comforted that Paul in these verses deals with the continual struggle that a Christian faces by trying to avoid sin. Paul knows this struggle but does not deal with it here. The passage deals with those who are separated from Christ, not those who are already united with Christ. The passage concerns those who serve themselves and not those who serve God in Christ Jesus. When people expect a reward from God for what they have done, Paul considers such an attitude a return to the power of sin over humanity.

The Spirit and the Flesh (8:1–17)

Paul has dealt extensively with all humanity under sin, the wrath of God, the interplay of law and sin, and the need for breaking the bondage of sin which has been accomplished through Christ. In this chapter he exultantly offers his reflection on the power of God through his Spirit. If chapter 7 was a view of the past from the Christian perspective, this chapter is a view of the present from that same perspective and continues the hope for the future. God accomplished through Christ and the Spirit what the law could not do: destroy the power of sin and fulfill the law in the Spirit.

These verses could be examined as living according to the Spirit and according to the flesh. We should begin by recalling that living by

Flesh	*Spirit*
self and self-accomplishments	God and relationship to God
merit and reward	love offered freely by God
idolatry of self-serving	serving others
law and sin	freedom of children of God

the flesh and the Spirit is not living according to two parts of human nature. Flesh designates a way of living in which the person concentrates on self and self-accomplishments and merit and reward. Living according to the Spirit is the same person who lives according to a new relationship with God, who accepts God's love not as demanded or expected or even as a reward, but as a free gift. This type of living frees a person from the idolatry of self-serving and also frees the person from the law and sin. This life is the life of the freedom of the children of God who has loved us first and reconciled all not on merit but as grace.

In this chapter Paul also uses the word "body" which signifies for him living as an individual in a physical world in relation to others. He could not envision human life apart from a body since he did not have the Greek understanding of body and soul. People living under sin lived bodily as individuals in relationship to this world and in relationship to each other. People living in the Spirit also live bodily as individuals in a physical world in relationship to others, but the manner of living differs. When he speaks of "flesh" rather than body, Paul refers not to the physical aspect of human life but rather to the living within the framework of sin and rebellion from God and alienation from God.

In Old Testament traditions there always lived the hope that people would live according to the law of God as coming from within rather than from without. Ezekiel described this as a new spirit:

A new heart I will give you, and a new spirit I will put within you and I will take out of your flesh the heart of stone and give you a heart of flesh. (Ez 36:26–27).

Paul may have had this in mind when he wrote of the fulfillment of the

Life in the flesh	Life in the Spirit
death	eternal life
hostility toward God	friendship with God
God's displeasure	God's forgiveness
strife with others	peace with others

law through the Spirit (8:4). The greater power of the Spirit of God has broken the old way of living according to the flesh, and now believers can live a new way of life according to the Spirit (8:4–5). Life in the flesh brought death, hostility toward God, and God's displeasure (8:6–8). Life lived according to the Spirit brings instead life and peace (8:6). Christians live according to the Spirit. They have abandoned their previous life of orientation to self and self-worth and self-acclaim and merit and not belonging to God alone (8:9). This Spirit will also give the promise of new life to come (8:11). And even though we continue to live in a world not yet fulfilled in the Spirit, we can experience this new life now and experience God's righteousness for us (8:10) while we await the fullness of life given to our mortal bodies by the risen Christ (8:11).

Abba

And so the Spirit brings us into the family of God. We can call God "Abba" (8:15), the term of endearment used by a child in the presence of a loving parent. People have been freed from the world of alienation from God (8:12), open to a new life in the Spirit which makes all children of God (8:14). The Spirit has transformed the slave to a child and then an heir (8:14–17). If Jesus is the true Son and we are members of God's family, then Jesus is brother (8:29) to all and all are sisters and brothers to Jesus. The whole world has been changed through the power of the Spirit, and people are liberated from relying only on themselves.

The Spirit and the Future (8:18–39)

Hope springs eternal. The passage of winter each year, the new birth in spring, the laughter of water in brooks and streams and lakes and even the ocean remind all peoples of the goodness of creation.

Winter has always been an image of pain and suffering, and spring has always been the symbol of new life and hope and better possibilities. "If winter comes, can spring be far behind?"

Suffering for Paul is the winter that people must experience before they share in the glory of spring, the glory of the renewed creation in God through Christ Jesus. The pain of the present means nothing in comparison to what Paul sees as the future (8:18). All of creation has been pained through the power of evil and sin. From the very beginning of the Bible in Genesis, people recognized that God's wonderful creation was out of line, things were not as they should have been, and so nature suffered just as humankind suffered. But now things were to be different (8:19–22). The groaning of creation will give way to the sharing in the glorious freedom of the children of God (8:21–22). The mountains will leap, the valleys will sing, the oceans will dance, the birds and animals and all created things will join the one glorious song and unite in the one glorious movement of joy as God restores what was lost. Humankind as the pinnacle of this created order also will be renewed and the groaning will give way to the full redemption of the body (8:23). All of God's children will experience the goodness and the value that God has freely given to be preserved, and the evil and sin will be destroyed forever. This is the hope that saves not just humanity but all of creation, and this hope of what is to come gives the patience, the courage to wait with longing, an expectation (8:24–25). The ecstatic Paul revels in what has happened to all of God's children and joyously looks to a glorious future for all of creation. All this God has accomplished through Christ and the Spirit.

Works of the Spirit

This same Spirit is ever present even in human weakness (8:26), ever anxious to intercede for us. In the past the faithful could not communicate with God and now they can. God has given the Spirit which makes it possible for all to unite with God even as they live in hope for the future (8:26–27). For we know that God works good for us (8:28), for he has called us and that is enough. People can live confidently. The end of humanity is redemption, the preservation of all that is good and the union of humankind with God forever. This destiny awaits not just some but all. God stands as the future of the human race and all of creation and God alone. All are destined to live like Jesus the first-born (8:29). This first-born now raised lives as the first-born among many, and those many will be included in the same destiny as Jesus. Humanity has been called in Jesus. Humanity can stand in God's presence. Humanity can share in the glory, the power and the goodness of God (8:30) because of what God has done and not because of anything humanity has done or not done.

And finally Paul has reached the pinnacle of his ecstasy, the summit of his exuberance for the power of the Spirit of God in human life: "If God is for us who is against us" (8:31)? This God has already given us his Son, and so there is nothing that this loving God will withhold from us (8:32). Three questions follow all of which bring a comforting answer:

Who can bring a charge against us? Surely not God for God has already justified us, has reconciled us, has allowed us to stand in his presence (8:33).

Who can condemn us? Surely not Christ who has already died for us and who now as risen Lord intercedes for us (8:34).

Who can separate us from the love of Christ? Absolutely nothing. Not pain and not sorrow, not need, not anything (8:35).

God is with us. God is with humanity. God is with creation. Nothing can be against us. Humanity is already the conqueror in Christ and the battle is over (8:37).

In verses 38 and 39 the summit has finally been reached. No creature can separate us from the love of God. We are saved finally from ourselves, for even people themselves cannot separate themselves and their world from God. God has so declared and God's word will not be nullified. The God of all is a God of love, and this God is for us, for all humanity, for all of creation. No one can be against this glorious reality of humankind. God has already given humanity Jesus. Nothing else matters. Nothing else remains to be done.

STUDY QUESTIONS

1. God is humankind's future. How does this affect the present?

2. God allows people to "stand in his presence" as a gift. How does this affect a person's self-image?

3. God justifies all without exception. Yet this does not mean that people can just do whatever they please. How are these ideas reconciled?

4. Why is Abraham such an important figure for Paul? Is Abraham an important figure in Christianity?

5. Christ has been the means by which God has accomplished peace, reconciliation and salvation. How was this accomplished? How does this affect Christian faith?

6. Does original sin make any sense today?

7. Baptism is the beginning of a process and is present in everyday life. Baptism finds completion only in death. What are the implications for this teaching?

8. Is Jesus really a kind master?

9. Can we ever do away completely with law?

10. How does the Spirit help people in their struggle with sin?

11. If grace overcomes all, then why do Christians still sin and have problems?

12. What future does the Spirit offer?

13. All of creation is suffering. All of creation will feel the power of redemption. What should Christians do as we await this full revelation?

Chapter 12

ISRAEL, CHRISTIANITY AND GOD'S GRACE

Suggested Scriptural Reading:

Romans 9–11

Traditionally scholars have debated the division of Romans, its unity, where the greeting ends, where the letter originally ended, the relationship among the various parts and how it fits into the general plan of Paul's theology as well as his actual reason for writing. In most cases no definitive answers are recognized even by the majority of scholars to all of these questions. One area, however, in which all scholars agree is that chapters 9–11 of the letter have a unity of their own and exist as a clear division. One scholar even analyzed the structure and detected parallels throughout the chapters with a general plan of positive attitudes toward Judaism in chapter 9, negative attitudes in chapter 10, and finally a return to positive attitudes in chapter 11. While not accepting such a carefully worked out structure as sometimes proposed, it seems to me that Paul did construct a careful argument in the relationship between Jews and Gentiles within the Christian church.

Preaching the gospel first to Jews in their own land was no historical accident. God would remain true to the promises and so the good news of salvation in Christ was first offered to Jews. They were the chosen people, shared in the glory of God, had been given the covenant and the law and the worship of the true God (9:4). These same people were descendants of the patriarchs and from them came Jesus the Christ (9:5). The gospel was preached first to Jews, and even if only a remnant responded (11:5), that remnant included Paul (11:1).

Of course it also included the Jerusalem church and also those members of the Roman church who had Jewish origins.

In this epistle Paul deals with the question of the collection for the Jerusalem church as we have already noted. We could say that following the analogy of the olive tree (11:17–24) the Gentiles have an obligation to the Jewish Christian community in Jerusalem and can respond to this obligation by assisting them in their need. The Jerusalem church continued the Jewish tradition into Christianity and thus they passed on a spiritual heritage to Gentiles. Now Gentiles could share in the rich spiritual tradition of Israel and in fact in themselves realized the destiny of the chosen people (11:2–7).

Such an appreciation of Jewish roots would also lead the Gentile Christians to respect those Jews who maintained a commitment to those roots. Even if Gentiles need not observe Jewish customs and traditions, they could not cut themselves off from any Jewish Christians, especially the mother church in Jerusalem. If they did, they would separate themselves from the olive tree onto which they had been grafted (11:17).

Paul wishes his readers to rethink their positions and appreciate the legitimacy of Israel's heritage in the Christian church. Paul has softened his position since Galatians. Now if some Jewish Christians want to continue a loyalty to Jewish practice and law, then they should be accepted by Gentile Christians who see no need for such practices. On their part, the Jewish Christians who are so inclined must realize that God had also chosen Gentiles in this church and they need not become Jews. Both groups relied completely on God's mercy and not on themselves and not on any practices.

If Gentile Christians or Jewish Christians harbored hostility toward those Jews who would not accept Christ and his gospel, they too were wrong. These Jews still remained part of the Jewish heritage given by God and they still embodied a spiritual heritage from which Christianity had developed.

God's Plan (9:1–33)

Paul has come to accept the reality that the majority of the Jews will not accept Christ. Such a thought caused considerable stress for him. He had come to see the blessings of Israel, the promises made of old, fulfilled in Christ Jesus. But if most of his fellow Jews have rejected this fulfillment, then they have frustrated God's promises and blessing. If God's plan has failed for Israel, then can it also fail in Christianity? Paul addresses this issue in chapter 9.

The word of God has not failed (9:6). He begins by sharing his own pain (9:1–3). Paul identifies himself as a Jew and would do anything for his fellow members of God's chosen people. From this chosen group has come the great spiritual heritage of law and glory and promises and worship and Jesus himself (9:4–5). No, the word of God has not failed, for true belonging to God's people is not based on biological descent (9:7–8) but upon God's continued gracious election in promise (9:8). God continues to choose, and often beyond what is expected. So the line continued through Isaac who was not Abraham's first-born (9:7). The same unexpected choice is made with Jacob rather than Esau (9:10–13). Isaac was chosen before birth, before he or Esau could have done anything. Election is God's choice and God's alone. God's decision to bless humanity through a chosen people cannot be frustrated if some refuse to share in the fulfillment of that promise in Christ.

In verse 14 Paul returns to a familiar phrase "What then (*to oun*) shall we say?" He had used it, as we have seen, in 6:1, 15 and 7:7. God continues to choose and show mercy and compassion to whom he wishes to show mercy and compassion (9:14–18). People have no say in how God operates, for God always remains God. He does no injustice. *Me genoita!* No way! (9:14). No one can tell God what to do or not to do. People's will or desire or activities can never demand anything from God. God chooses people for his own purpose. God shows mercy or hardens hearts, and no one can call God to account (9:20), for God is God (9:17–18).

Predestination

Some may think that verses 21–29 deal with predestination or, more accurately, predetermination. They do involve the former but not in the sense that every individual is determined in a pre-set manner. Their destiny is determined, and that destiny for humanity is God, both Jew and Gentile. How individuals reach that destiny is not part of the determined plan. Whether everyone actually reaches that destiny is also beyond Paul's thought. He deals with Israel and with humanity. Both will be fulfilled in God's plan of salvation. Paul is not dealing with any particular individual. Even when he deals with vessels of wrath made for destruction (9:22), he does not say that they are destroyed. Rather, God bears with them with patience to reveal his mercy, and Paul refers to both Jews and Gentiles (9:24). Who knows what God's mercy and grace has in store even for those vessels of wrath? Surely Paul knows the danger that exists for any individual who refuses to accept the gracious gift of God. God may actually honor that choice. But such a refusal is not the result of God's decision or activity. People make that choice. And no one knows the depth of God's mercy.

God will choose from among the peoples of the world to be his chosen ones, his beloved (9:25–29). God will not allow his promises to be lost, for a remnant will remain to fulfill the word of God (9:27). In these verses Paul returns to the very words of Jewish scriptures to emphasize how God will move beyond the chosen people of Israel, as he has done for the Gentiles, and that his promises will be fulfilled even if not all accept their destiny. God will remain God, free to do as God wills, but always this God acts with mercy, compassion and grace, affording redemption to all, Jew and Gentile. Each has only to accept the gift.

"What shall we say?" (9:30). God has offered his grace to Gentiles even though they did not pursue it, and they have accepted through faith (9:30). The Jews made the mistake of trying to accomplish righteousness in the sight of God through observance of the law, and they have failed (9:31–32). They have stumbled over their own efforts to make themselves right in the sight of God. Instead of accepting in faith, as did Abraham, they relied on the law and the law itself became the stumbling block. The law became sin for them as they trusted in themselves. They wanted to tell God they were righteous because of what they had personally accomplished. They stumbled. With this Paul begins some negative comments on his fellow Jews.

Failure and God's Fidelity (10:1–13)

Once Israel set out to merit God's righteousness, God's grace, they failed. They stumbled not because they were not religious, not because they did not follow the law, but because they did not understand the law. They surely had a zeal (10:2) but it was self-centered. They wished to establish their own righteousness. They failed to submit to the righteousness of Christ (10:3). Christ alone fulfills the law, and people will then fulfill the law when they accept him in faith (10:4). In the past people trusted to have the right relationship with God through the law, but now the right relationship with God comes from Christ and him alone.

God remains faithful to all of his creation. Now this faithfulness

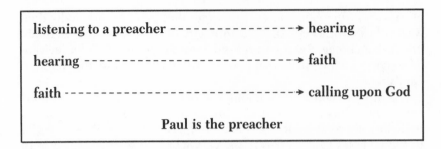

becomes fulfilled in Christ. In verses 6–13 Paul interprets several verses of Deuteronomy and brings them up to date by applying an explanation to suit the contemporary scene and need (midrash). Moses had assured the people that the law of God is easily accessible to them (10:8). Now this law is actually fulfilled in Christ, and so he alone is the way to God and not the law. Paul accepted in faith the events of the life of Christ as expressing God's faithfulness, especially as seen in the raising of Jesus from the dead (10:9). God overcame death for Jesus and now people can trust God through faith in Jesus (10:9–10). The one God is God of all peoples, and no distinction exists among Jews and Gentiles (10:12). If all people only trust in God, they will be saved from evil and sin and death (10:13). People can never be disappointed if they so act (10:11).

Preaching the Word (10:14–21)

The principal verse in this passage is verse 17: "Faith comes from what is heard, and what is heard comes from the preaching of Christ." God has commissioned Paul to preach the word of Christ. God has given Paul this awesome responsibility and Paul will not waver in his efforts to preach that word. The gospel is not read but proclaimed and heard. Paul would proclaim and his audience was the Gentiles. The logic in verses 14–15 is clear: Calling upon God depends upon faith, faith comes from hearing, and hearing comes from listening to a preacher. Paul is the preacher calling for faith so that people may call upon God for his mercy and grace. Some respond and some do not (10:16).

Paul concludes this chapter by building his case against those who failed to hear. They both heard and understood (10:18–19). Paul includes in his arguments quotations from Psalm 19:4 and Deuteronomy 32:31. Moreover, Isaiah himself acknowledged other people than Jews accepting God (10:20), and faithful Jews should have recognized this coming of Gentiles as part of God's plan. Instead they refused to accept what God had done for both Jews and Gentiles and failed to trust in the gracious goodness of God for all peoples. They hardened their hearts and fulfilled the words of Isaiah: "All day long I have held out my hands to a disobedient and contrary people" (10:21; Is 65:2). What a terrible way to end his thoughts on the chosen people Israel! But that is not how Paul's thought ends.

God and the Future for All (11:1–36)

God brought disobedience upon humanity so that God could show his grace to all humanity (11:32). In many ways this chapter concludes all that has preceded and prepares for the following chapters that have more to do with behavior and activity. The letter began with Israel as God's chosen and concludes with Israel again, but now it is the relationship that exists between Israel as God's chosen people and the new Israel, the church of Christ Jesus.

All humanity has shared a common lot of sin and wrath (3:23). Now all humanity has the possibility of redemption through Christ (3:24). All of creation will share in this redemption (8:19–23). We might be tempted to try to sort things out, to divine the mind of God, but all such efforts are useless. Paul seems to have known well the meaning of the old Portuguese proverb: "God writes straight with crooked lines." Or perhaps he understood well the oriental image of God's plan as the reverse side of a hand-stitched oriental rug which will be revealed only when the rug is completed and turned over to see the pattern and the beauty. We may try but we will fail to understand the thought of God, for God's thoughts are not ours and his ways not ours. The chapter concludes with another of Paul's ecstatic outbursts which ring with their own power apart from any comment:

Oh the depth of the riches and wisdom and knowledge of God. How unsearchable are his judgments and how inscrutable his ways. For who has known the mind of the Lord, or who has been his counselor. Or who has given a gift to him that he might be repaid. For from him and through him and to him are all things. To him glory forever. Amen (11:33–36).

Paul begins with Israel and God's plan (11:1–11). Has God re-

---

rejection by Israel - - - - - - - - - - - ➤ reconciliation of the world

acceptance - - - - - - - - - - - - ➤ life from the dead

---

jected his people? *Me genoita!* No way! Paul is a Jew and he continues to share that heritage. In this apostle, God surely has not rejected his people. Moreover Paul cites the historical example of Elijah (11:2–3). When the prophet had thought that God had abandoned his people, God assured the prophet that a remnant remained and so God's promises would continue. The remnant remained for Elijah (11:4), and a remnant remains now in Christ (11:5). In both instances God chose, based not upon works but through grace (11:6).

Israel, Now and in the Future

What has happened to Israel? They have been hardened and Paul admits it (11:7–10). The question remains: Why did God do such a thing to his chosen and does God stand ready to condemn his chosen ones? *Me genoita!* No way! Have they stumbled so as to fall (11:1)? *Me genoita!* No way! Something bad has happened to Israel, and Paul admits it, but they have not fallen. Paul reflects here on actual experience. When the early preachers found opposition among the Jews they turned to the Gentiles, and the Gentiles responded. Paul himself had been sent specifically to preach to the Gentiles. In fact, by now in the experience of Paul more Gentiles had accepted this new way of faith in Christ than Jews, and the sure signs are that such a phenomenon will continue. But where does that leave Israel? Paul believes that when the Jews see the people who have accepted Christ, a Jew, they will become envious of the grace of God freely given to Gentiles and they themselves will become part of the new chosen people of God (11:11). The following verse presents Paul's hopes for the future based on what has already happened:

> Now if their trespass means riches for the world, and if their failure means riches for the Gentiles, how much more will their full inclusion mean (11:11).

For Paul full inclusion must go far beyond the blessings that have already taken place. He will return to this theme in verse 15 in which Paul states that the inclusion of the Jews in this new chosen people will bring life from the dead.

For if their rejection means reconciliation of the world, what
will their acceptance mean but life from the dead? If the
dough offered as first fruits is holy, so is the whole lump; and
if the root is holy so are the branches (11:15–16).

Paul addresses the Gentiles in these verses. He wants to help
them to realize the heritage they have received from the Jews. He
tries to lead them never to forget their indebtedness and thus offer
acceptance and tolerance of Jews who are Christian and maintain
certain Jewish practices. Paul is the apostle to the Gentiles and he can
tell them what he wants (11:13).

The Olive Tree

The analogy of the olive tree (11:17–24), a favorite image and a
favorite tree in Israel, explains well the thoughts of Paul. God gives
his grace freely but people may never presume on God's grace. The
tree is clearly God's people. The wild branches grafted on are the
Gentiles. When in the future the Jews, who have been cut off by their
rejection of Christ, are grafted upon the tree, it will be on the same
basis as the Gentiles, through grace and not through anything they do
of themselves.

The Gentiles may not boast but should stand in awe of what God
has done for them (11:18–20). Moreover these new branches which
were wild should be careful to remain in the kindness of God or they
will find themselves also cut off (11:21–22). The Jews remain chosen
and not completely abandoned. God can surely graft them to the
place where they belong. They were first (11:23–24). The olive tree
analogy expresses the purpose of God for all creation: the mercy of
God for all, even those who have, in the mind of Paul, "temporarily"
been cut off.

God plans and offers grace for all, both Jew and Gentile. Mercy is
for all (11:32). Paul speaks of God's plan as a mystery. Previously we
noted that by such terminology Paul implies that we understand only
something and never all until it is completed (11:33–36). Israel's
rejection is temporary until the Gentiles are all included and then all
of Israel will be saved (11:25–26). Isaiah 59:20–21 also has the sure
hope that God in his great mercy will forgive all because God is God.
Paul shares the same hope.

And he will come to Sion as redeemer, to those in Jacob who
turn from transgression, says the Lord. And as for me this is

my covenant with them says the Lord: my spirit which is upon you, and my words which I have put in your mouth, shall not depart out of your mouth, or out of the mouth of your children, or out of the mouth of your children's children, says the Lord, from this time forth and forevermore (Is: 59:20–21).

The Jews still have election. They are beloved and the gifts and call of God are irrevocable (11:28–29). Ultimately God's mercy will be evident for all. The Gentiles were outside and now are within because of God's mercy. The Jews who are outside now will also be invited within, all because of God's mercy. The disobedience by Israel is a temporary setback but only temporary. The Jews remain God's chosen people and always will remain so. They belong more so than Gentiles, and Gentiles can never boast of anything, for all is grace. Of course the great Christian tragedy is that often in the history of Christianity these chapters of Romans were forgotten. Perhaps some of the negative verses were taken out of context and the proclamation that the Jews remain God's beloved forever was overlooked. For whatever reasons, how unfortunate for the relationship between Christians and Jews.

For Paul Jewish Christians and Gentile Christians in the church of Rome must get along with love and acceptance, for all are under the same gracious decree of God which has brought salvation to all. Sin and law and death are gone. Life and grace abound now. Since the future is God alone the future must be good.

Oh the depth of the riches and wisdom and knowledge of God . . . from him and through him and to him are all things. To him be glory forever (11:33, 36).

Paul has finished his presentation to this community at Rome and now can offer his suggestions on how this community might live.

STUDY QUESTIONS

1. Why are chapters 9–11 often forgotten in Christianity?

2. Why do problems between Jews and Christians persist? Why has anti-semitism been so strong in Christianity?

3. The Jews are God's chosen people. What does this mean for Judaism, for Christianity, and for people's image of God?

4. Gentiles are late-comers. What should characterize contemporary Christians in light of Romans 9–11?

5. What has disturbed you, haunted you, helped you in these chapters?

6. God is always faithful. What does this mean to the ordinary believer?

7. The future for all is good, for the future is God. How do the traditional images of hell and damnation and judgment fit within this framework?

8. Why does Paul wax so eloquently in his concluding thoughts? How is this part of his personality?

Chapter 13

THE LIVING OF GRACED BELIEVERS

Suggested Scriptural Reading:

Romans 12–16

Frequently when contemporary commentators on Romans treat these chapters they consider them general exhortations to the Roman community. The question remains whether the letter to the Romans, and in particular these exhortations, are specifically directed to one church or are general admonitions that are suitable for all church communities. Many commentators on Paul also analyze his letters under a general framework of doctrinal exposition followed by moral directives. Under such a division, the first eleven chapters of Romans contain the doctrinal presentation, and these chapters are the moral directives. So we may consider these chapters: general exhortations to the church at Rome; general exhortations to all churches and not written specifically to Rome, or also just the usual method that Paul uses in first presenting some doctrinal teaching and then offering some moral directives. Another possibility exists. I believe the whole letter was written to the church at Rome with these chapters specific exhortations to that particular community.

Paul's Purpose in Writing Letters

Paul did not set out to write a compendium of theology. Nor did he even attempt a systematic presentation of the life, ministry, death and resurrection of Jesus as we find in the gospels. Paul preached the gospel of the risen Lord. When he chose to write a letter, such re-

---

The general format of Paul's letters: doctrine -------→ moral

General exhortations --------→ to the Roman church

General exhortations --------→ to all churches

Specific exhortations--------→ to the Roman church

---

sulted from particular needs. His letters are occasional in nature and should be understood in light of the particular community to which he addressed his thoughts.

Certainly Romans was an unusual letter since he was writing to a church he had not founded. We would expect Paul to have a slightly different approach but not so different as to change the general purpose he had in writing letters.

Rather than see these chapters as some general moral exhortations, they should be seen rather as responding to the particular needs of the Roman community. Paul could have chosen to write a general treatise on Christian living, but he wrote rather appropriately to the churches in Rome. We can read through these chapters and discover how Paul attempted to deal with the peculiar circumstances facing the Christians in Rome.

The need for unity in the Christian church weighed heavily on Paul. Christianity should not be divided into Jewish and Gentile Christianity according to his thinking. Moreover, Jewish roots should be preserved even if Gentiles could feel freedom from Jewish observance. The complex situation of the Roman churches demanded some delicate balancing. To this need Paul responded first in his presentation on the meaning of the gospel of grace and then in these chapters on the implications for the Roman community coming from this one gospel of grace.

Relationships of Chapters 12–15

"By God's mercy" (12:1) links this chapter to chapter 11 (11:30) and sets the basic theme for the moral exhortations that will follow. At the end of verse 2 Paul exhorts his readers to renew their minds: "that you may prove what is the will of God." All have to learn the will of

God and respond accordingly. They will begin by not thinking too highly of themselves but think and thus act, according to faith. Both Jewish and Gentile Christians have to discern the will of God. They have to learn to view each other in a new way and will do so by putting on Christ (13:14). Above all they must learn to discover the will of God both in regard to the Jewish roots of Christianity and the question of Jewish observance. What might be considered as general exhortations in these chapters becomes specific in regard to the Roman churches.

The warning against thinking too highly of oneself (12:3) has particular reference to those who considered themselves above Jewish observance. And the measure of one's faith should not be judged according to the degree in which Jewish observance is accepted or not. This would apply to both strong and weak.

The remarks on unity (12:4–5) are also well suited to a divided church. Even the gifts spoken of in verses 6–8 are not general exhortations but are chosen not at random but to suit the problems facing the Roman churches. Prophecy, service and teaching are involved. These particular gifts responded to problems for the Romans. Prophets can declare the will of God whether strong or weak, provided each prophecy comes from faith. Service may well refer to the collection for the Jerusalem church. If they will be of service they should not pick and choose whom they will serve. Teachers would be particularly in difficult straits, for they are expected to declare what is acceptable and what is not acceptable to a divided community. Rather than some general gifts, Paul chose those gifts needed for the Roman churches.

The references to love of one's fellow Christian (12:10) and mutual respect, living in harmony (12:9–21), are all suited to the Roman community which needed to overcome their divisions and recognize the power of the mercy of God for all.

Chapter 13 deals with some questions on the relationship to Roman authorities (13:1–7) and then with Jewish law (13:8–10). In the discussion of the former we have already noted that Jews and thus Jewish Christians had troubles with the authorities by causing disturbances. If some Jewish Christians claimed that Gentiles could stand equally in the presence of God without observance of Jewish law (Paul's position), this would cause trouble within the Jewish community, which in turn would cause civil disturbances. Christians needed to live in harmony with all.

If two groups exist side by side, one observing Jewish law and the other claiming that it was not necessary, relations could easily become unloving. Love alone fulfills the law (13:8-10).

Chapters 14 and 15 deal with specific issues of the weak and the strong and suit specific concerns of the Roman community. All must be accepted in the community, Jew and Gentile alike. All must live in harmony with mutual respect. God's will includes both Jew and Gentile. All have received mercy and so no one can put himself or herself above the other. These chapters are not just some general observations after a long presentation of doctrine but specific responses to specific problems in the Roman churches.

Life in Christ (12:1-21)

Christians must renew their minds, their thinking and their doing on the basis of faith. The living sacrifice (12:1) is the offering of a life well lived. It is spiritual worship, for this then is offered in their worship. Such a sacrifice involves doing and in particular discovering the will of God (12:2).

The spiritual sacrifice involves accepting oneself and not taking pride (in what would be Jewish observance or the freedom of not observing Jewish practices) (12:3). Each one has a gift and each gift contributes to the community, whether that gift is prophecy or teaching or service or exhortation (12:4-8). These gifts are particularly important for the Roman community. Above all let love characterize your relationships within the community (12:9-13) and even toward those who persecute you (12:14-21).

Each verse can make sense if Paul is writing to a divided community seeking harmony and reconciliation. They will need to be patient in tribulation (12:12), live in harmony, and never be conceited (12:16). Repay evil with good (12:21). Hold no grudges (12:19). Treat your enemies as your friends (12:14,20). Put in the context of this community as presented earlier, each admonition strikes home.

The State (13:1-7)

Harmony within the community also demands harmony without. Christians have to live in peace with authorities. These verses may have in mind a particular historical situation. In 58 C.E. Tacitus describes a rebellion against indirect taxation and Nero was forced to intervene. Rather than abolish such taxes the emperor mitigated them and sought to control the greed of the collectors. Paul would have been writing his letter at the time when this problem would be coming to a head. Not only does this show his acute knowledge of the situation at Rome, but it also gives us further insights into his thought in such matters. Christians do not contribute to social disorder. When taxes are due, then they are paid (13:6–7). Civil authorities also serve and so demand respect (13:4, 1–2).

Love (13:8–10)

Paul now turns to the keeping of the Jewish law. Love alone fulfills the law (13:8, 10). The keeping of the commandments, of which Paul mentions four, are good in themselves, but are all related to the fundamental law which is the love of one's neighbor. Whether the Christian deals with civil authorities or members of one's own community, law makes sense only when it is the manifestation of love. Without the love, the law means nothing and in fact is not observed. If Paul faced a situation in which some claimed to be observing the law and failed to show love to a fellow Christian, he responds bluntly: The law is fulfilled when you love your neighbor.

Act in Love (13:11–14)

The conclusion sums up all of these moral exhortations: "Put on the Lord Jesus Christ" (13:14). Salvation is present and is coming, and so the only appropriate action is love (13:11). The works of darkness must be cast off (reveling, drunkenness, debauchery, licentiousness, quarreling and jealousy—v. 13) and works of the day must be put on. No doubt the Roman church had its quarrels and jealousies. Whether the other vices mentioned here are specific to this community or not remains unknown. Certainly at Rome in that period drunkenness and licentiousness were rather common. Whether Paul had heard that some of the Roman community still engaged in such activities we will never know with certainty. If, however, Paul had such knowledge of the Roman community as was seen in his awareness of the indirect taxes, then we might presume that these sins also are not just a general laundry list but specific issues which have come to him. Again, this would suit the times at Rome and shows Paul's accurate knowledge of the community to which he writes.

The Weak and the Strong (14:1-12)

The precise identity of the two groups mentioned in these chapters, the weak (14:1) and the strong (15:1), will remain in dispute. They range from strict Judaizers to libertine Gentiles, vegetarians or even individuals involved in mystery cults. Also weak and strong can be used for all, depending on which side one finds oneself. To the strict observant Jewish Christian the weak are the Gentiles who fail to observe the law. To the more liberal Gentile Christian the weak are those who stick to the law. No matter who these groups are, Paul does deal with specific practices and ultimately calls for all to live in peace (14:19). Paul himself seems to say the weak are the Judaizers and the strong are the Gentile Christians free from law (15:1). This however may not be how the Judaizers looked upon themselves. He will identify with these free from law but will not abuse that freedom to cause problems for others (14:4, 13, 20; 15:1, 2, 7). Paul has come a long way from the time he wrote Galatians. He has mellowed and is willing to compromise for the sake of the unity of the gospel. All others should be willing to do the same.

Eating, Drinking, and Feasts

Two practices are involved here, and both are concerned with Jewish observance: rules for eating and drinking and the celebration of feasts. We know from Philo that some Jews in the diaspora abstained from both meat and wine although these are not strictly forbidden by Jewish law. Such ascetic practices were not commonplace but existed. For Paul to make specific reference to such practice in Romans might well indicate that some in Rome followed this strict Jewish ascetical practice going beyond the demands of the law. Some Gentile Christians who wanted to follow the example of their fellow Jewish Christians might have adopted the same custom and eaten only vegetables (14:2). The Paul of Galatians might have written differently, but the Paul of Romans says to let them alone. In their turn, those who choose to eat only vegetables should leave other Christians alone. It really does not matter.

As to the observance of feasts (14:5) the same is true. If some observe feasts and others do not, if some abstain and others do not, this should not cause problems in the community (14:5-6). All live in the Lord and that is sufficient for all (14:7-9). Do not pass judgment on any of these practices, and then we will be able to stand before the judgment of God and render an account on how we have rendered worship (the spiritual sacrifice of a good life?) and not on observance or non-observance (14:10–12). How Paul has changed!

Live in Harmony (14:13–23)

Live peacefully and be willing to compromise and overlook issues which are not important. Begin by not passing judgment (14:13). Why cause problems when you need not (14:13)? I may know that nothing is unclean, but if my neighbor chooses to maintain some Jewish practice, then why not (14:14)? Do not rub your brother's or sister's face in the mud by your liberal attitude, for they are your brothers and sisters and Christ died for all (14:15–16). The real meaning of the gospel is not what you eat or what you do not eat but being right in the presence of God and living in peace. Work for that and avoid causing problems for others (14:17–21). Live your own faith and make sure it is faith. You who still wonder about whether or not you can eat this or that, do not eat it, but follow what you think comes from faith (14:23).

All Belong (15:1–12)

Those who think they are freed from the law should also keep in mind those who think differently and try to please each other (15:12). Christ is the example, and he would wish all to live in harmony and thus glorify God his Father (15:3–6). Christ the Jew, the servant to the circumcised (15:7), fulfilled the promises to the patriarchs and now the Gentiles glorified God (15:8–12). Paul has concluded by his appeal to the law itself explaining how the Gentiles belong, and if they do not observe Jewish practices, they must not be excluded from the community.

Paul's Personal Remarks (15:13–33)

The letter began with an introduction of personal remarks and concludes with a long section of personal remarks dealing with what Paul has accomplished as a missionary (15:14–21), and with his plans for the future (15:22–23). He believes that the Romans possess goodness and knowledge (15:14), but also as the apostle to the Gentiles he has written boldly (15:15–16). What he has done has been good and Paul will not be ashamed of it (15:17–22). He is the apostle for all the

Gentiles and he will fulfill that responsibility. Included is his mission to bring about a unity among Jewish and Gentile Christians. Although he will not build on another's foundation (15:20) he chose to respond to the Roman community because of his responsibility as apostle to the Gentiles.

His future plans call for a visit to Rome, then to Spain, but first a visit to Jerusalem (15:22–25). Here Paul mentions the collection. Other Gentile communities have given generously to the church in Jerusalem because of the spiritual heritage (15:25–27). Before he will arrive in Rome he asks not for a contribution to the collection but for their prayers (15:30). He needs the support of this community as he begins a troublesome trip and presumes on their welcoming him when he arrives (15:31–33).

The Ending (16:1–27)

For centuries the authenticity of this chapter has been discussed. We have some manuscripts which end at chapter 15, others at chapter 14 and then others, of course, which include chapter 16. The opinion that Romans was a general letter which was made specific by the addition of Rome in chapter 1, and this concluding chapter has always found some advocates. The problem of so many names listed (there are twenty-six) seems odd. How could he have known so many Christians in Rome and why did he name them all? But if he wanted to be accepted, would he not name as many names as possible?

I believe the better solution is to accept the unity of the letter as it is. This chapter belongs, and the letter was sent to Rome.

The first twenty-three verses are a long list of names, all associates of Paul and all apparently known in the Roman community. The letter ends with a long benediction (16:25–27). Glory forevermore be to God through Jesus Christ. Glory be to this same one God who revealed his mystery of obedience in faith for all nations—revealed first in the prophets and now through the preaching of the gospel of Jesus Christ. It is finished. Now Paul awaits the outcome.

STUDY QUESTIONS

1. Do you think Paul knew the Romans' situation well or not?

2. Do you think the tendency of contemporary exegetes to act like

sleuths in analyzing every word and possible condition helps in understanding the New Testament?

3. Why are warnings necessary? Do they fit the general tone of the letter?

4. How should a Christian relate to state problems today?

5. Is life in Christ really as easy as Paul seems to imply?

6. Who do you think are the weak and the strong? Are they present in the church today? What are you? How do you respond to others who differ from your position?

7. Unity and harmony are all-important. Why?

8. What do you like best about Romans? Is your thinking different on Romans than on Galatians?

SECTION IV

Pauline Theology

Chapter 14

THE NEW COMMUNITY OF FAITH

Paul the rugged individualist loved community and gave of himself to establish, nourish and protect the early Christian communities. If Israel could make sense only as a gathering of God's people, for Paul the new Israel could make sense only if the individual believers banded together as one. The primary object of his missionary work was community. In both Galatians and Romans, Paul writes first to a community he founded and then to a community which he wanted to visit and from which he wanted support. The individual believers became stronger as they united with a common faith. Paul wanted them to be strong and live in peace and in love, founded on a faith that offered deliverance.

Christianity Means Community

Christianity survives on the members living in mutual dependence. Such a prospect does not imply a weakness but rather a sense of power and strength. People need other people, and Paul himself recognized this in his special affection for the Philippians. Even when he is harsh in Galations, his motivation is love. God has created people for community and thus only together can people fulfill their destiny and reach their fulfillment.

Paul certainly experienced the risen Lord in his journey to Damascus. His life changed radically. But Paul could continue in this new way of living only if he was sustained by the support and love and guidance of other believers. He may have located his new being in an identity with the risen Lord, but this Lord lived among the community and did not always dramatically intervene as Paul had experienced once on the road to Damascus.

Community of Faith and Love

To understand Paul's theology demands an appreciation of how he saw others as members of a community of faith. Since the new community had its roots in Judaism, Paul and other Christians had to rethink their commitment to the old traditions and somehow bring them in line with their new commitment to Jesus. This Paul outlined in both Galations and Romans. In many ways Romans was Paul's effort to reinterpret his religious past. The earlier Paul could never have viewed Israel and the law as the traditions in the same manner as the Christian Paul.

Paul not only accepted this new life but wanted people to actually live it. If grace and freedom and justification were more than just forensic declarations, then somehow people had to experience their power. They did this when love became the binding force in the community. If God had taken care of people, pardoning, forgiving and calling them blameless, then people could take care of each other. People could pardon and forgive and consider each other blameless. Such was his ardent desire in Romans.

One Another

Throughout Romans, Paul makes frequent use of the reciprocal pronoun: "Love one another with brotherly affection" (Rom 12:10). "Live in harmony with one another" (Rom 12:16). "Outdo one another in showing honor" (Rom 12:10). "May the God of steadfastness and encouragement grant you to agree with one another in accord with Christ Jesus" (Rom 15:5). "Let us no more pass judgment on one another" (Rom 14:13). "Welcome one another, therefore, as Christ has welcomed you" (Rom 15:7). "I myself am satisfied about you, my brethren, that you yourselves are full of goodness, filled with all knowledge, and able to instruct one another" (Rom 15:14). "Greet one another with a holy kiss" (Rom 16:16).

All of these come from the last section of Romans, the section directed specifically to the churches at Rome but also applicable to all Christian communities. Certainly the notion of "one another" figures prominently in the mind of Paul. The new community involves a com-

- love one another
- outdo one another
- agree with one another
- do not pass judgment on one another
- welcome one another
- instruct one another
- greet one another

mon life in every way, with peace and joy and freedom and unity and equality.

Diversity in Unity

Within this community of faith, Paul also accepts the diversity of talents and gifts. Some are Greeks, others Jews. The community has its share of the strong and the weak, the slave and the free, male and female. If, however, God has justified all, then a fundamental equality distinguishes this community. People are equal in the eschatological community, and this equality must be expressed in the present community. Such equality, however, does not destroy distinctions within the community. Paul himself is a leader and teacher and he expects people to listen to him and obey him. He does not concern himself here with the elimination of all differences within the community and its specific roles, but with the elimination of values associated with the roles. In fact since for society roles can be used to dominate and even oppress, the roles within this community serve rather as functions: some are teachers, others prophets or healers or administrators. Such service functions do not negate the fundamental equality.

Equality for All

Perhaps no passage from Paul is more famous than his declaration of equality in Galatians. Nor has many passages in Paul caused so much discussion.

For as many of you as were baptized into Christ have put on Christ. There is neither Jew nor Greek, there is neither slave

nor free, there is neither male nor female; for you are all one
in Christ Jesus (Gal 3:27–28).

Recent research indicates that Paul has incorporated here an early
baptismal formula. This gives us an insight not only into Paul's
thought but also into the meaning of baptism, at least in the Pauline
churches.

In a world that more frequently separates than unites, Paul's use
of this formula comforts a divided society. Too often people experience separation by sex, by race, by education, by social position, by
family origins, and today differs little from the time of Paul. In the
new way of living, any values based only on differences give way. The
community of Jesus accepts all as equals. In specifically enumerating
the three great distinctions of the ancient world, Paul effectively does
away with all superior-inferior relationships.

Slavery

Contemporary Christians usually applaud Paul for his declaration. He fought constantly for the equality of Jew and Gentile in the
Christian community without any need for the Gentile to submit to
any aspect of the law. The question of slavery was not settled by early
Christianity. No one need belabor that. But at least within the community of believers it seems that slaves and masters were considered
equal. The presence of the letter to Philemon in the New Testament
offers sufficient attestation to that position. Onesimus seems to have
stolen from Philemon, and yet Paul convinces the slave to return. If
we read between the lines, Paul suggests that Philemon offer Onesimus his freedom. Such would be the natural outcome of the meaning
of equality in baptism as expressed in Galatians. The almost side matter of the stolen property seems to take for granted that the master
will forgive this transgression. This also suits the general thought of
both Galatians and Romans.

Equality of the Sexes

When we come to the question of the equality of the sexes, however, contemporary Christians usually do not believe that Paul accepted that equality. Some have even labeled Paul a male chauvinist.
If such were the case, then Paul repudiates the very basis of his theology declared specifically in Galatians.

To study the thought of Paul in the equality of the sexes, we can begin by excluding those epistles which are at least questionable with regard to Pauline authorship: Ephesians, Colossians, 1 and 2 Timothy and Titus. Many of the usual references to Paul's chauvinism are in secondary letters. Some need careful explanation. The reference to 1 Corinthians 14:33b–35 in which women are admonished to keep silent in church assemblies seems odd.

As in all the churches of the saints, the women should keep silence in the churches. For they are not permitted to speak but should be subordinate as even the law says. If there is anything they desire to know, let them ask their husbands at home. For it is shameful for a woman to speak in church (1 Cor 14:33b–35).

Just previous to this Paul had stated that women not only can ask questions but they can also preach and pray publicly: "Any woman who prays or prophesies. . ." (1 Cor 11:5a). One plausible explanation to the remark in 1 Corinthians 14 is that it is an insertion. Someone, sometime, added this verse for whatever reasons. Although this argument might seem specious, the addition of verses in the New Testament by later hands seems rather common. No matter what, it is surely foreign to his notion of equality and does not fit the previous verses in Corinthians.

Of course, the larger question is 1 Corinthians 11:2–16 itself. Herein Paul argues strenuously that women leading worship (praying and prophesying) must cover their heads. Paul does not exclude women from participation in the church, but rather, following the custom of the times, he maintains the distinction between the sexes. Women cover their heads and men do not. Even the reference to Christ as the head in verse 3 has two possibilities. Head, *kephale* in Greek, can mean metaphorically "ruler" or "source." The latter fits the meaning of this verse. Christ is the source of man and man is the source of woman according to the Jewish tradition in Genesis 2. This may not satisfy everyone, but it at least raises some question about the interpretation of the man as the one with authority over the woman. The previous interpretation would be contrary to what Paul has preached and what he has encouraged. I do not believe Paul was the great male chauvinist as he has often been portrayed.

Just as the Christians in the late first century lacked the courage to live out Paul's doctrine of justification by faith, so they also betrayed these views of egalitarianism. The so-called household codes in Colossians 3:18–4:1, Ephesians 5:21–6:9 and 1 Timothy 2:8–15 contain the only instances in the New Testament in which women are explicitly subordinated to man. Paul surely knew of these formulas in Greek culture but chose not to use them. They did not fit into his understanding of grace and freedom and equality. If the later church incorporated them into the canon and even associated them with the authority of Paul, we should still return to Galatians and Romans to understand the fundamental teaching of Paul. The new community has already been blessed and forgiven and declared just in the sight of God. Who could possibly then begin to divide the community into superior and inferior? Paul surely modified his teaching from Galatians to Romans, but this fundamental gospel remained inviolate. All people, Jew or Greek, male or female, slave or free, had been justified by the goodness of God. They could stand in God's presence with their dignity because of what God had given them. Thus they will stand with each other in the church.

Receptive in Faith

With all of the emphasis on God's gifts to humankind, some may get the idea that people are merely passive. Paul says no. They are actively receptive in faith. Usually people understand faith as what a person believes, or how a person believes. Often enough faith becomes closer to an intellectual quality, and thus we say: "I accept it on faith." For Paul, faith is the fundamental position of humankind before the God who has already declared justification by grace. Faith is confidence, assurance that God has given new life. Faith remains steadfast in that same position even when anxiety or fear wants to rely on personal achievement. Faith is the attitude of a believer before God, conscious of good and bad, hope and despair, acceptance and rejection, but still standing there with dignity before the God who loved in sin and declared the individual and humanity blameless in Christ Jesus.

Faith is salvation now. Faith involves the experience of God present in one's life taking away the cynicism, the pessimism, the lack of direction, the isolation and the sense of being alone. Faith brings a sense of well-being and happiness and delight in world, in self and others. Faith brings a saving presence of God which helps the believer to maintain courage and hope and live with the firm conviction that God has already expressed much love.

The gift, however, has to be accepted. God does not force. Peo-

---

FAITH

- the fundamental position of people before God
- confidence in God
- assurance of the gift of new life
- steadfastness overcoming anxiety and fear
- conscious of good and bad, hope and despair
- standing with dignity
- declared blameless
- salvation now
- overcoming cynicism and pessimism
- a sense of well-being and happiness and delight
- courage and hope in a living God
- content with self, others and the world
                      because
- God has loved all in Christ Jesus

---

ple must open their hands to receive a gift. Standing with hands folded precludes any possibility of receiving. People actively receive the offer of God. Some associate faith with obedience but not with the notion of obeying commandments. Rather, obedience is a willingness to live in the presence of a God who has given life freely. Living in that posture is obedience. A provident God stands already present and people acknowledge that presence.

In Romans 4, Paul offers an example of faith in Abraham. This father of Judaism lived in the presence of a provident God willing to give up his past and follow this God from his homeland, willing to give up his future in his son when God asks for the sacrifice. Abraham trusted in this one God in the presence of the contrary. When everything says not to trust, Abraham trusted. Abraham is a model of faith. The confidence which was viewed as unwarranted becomes warranted.

Freedom

With such faith, people can live in freedom and peace and joy. People are free from restraint and sin and death and past history and failure and despair and law and regulations. "For freedom Christ has set us free; stand fast and do not submit again to a yoke of slavery"

(Gal 5:1). More than anything else people are free from trying to fulfill an impossible task, free from a tyranny of performance and value based on merit and free from rules and regulations that claim salvation. Free from the fear of going to hell because we did not do what we should have done. Free from fear and anxiety.

In Romans, Paul encourages all by his statement: "Let everyone be fully convinced in his own mind" (Rom 14:5). Let one choose for oneself how a person can live in the presence of a provident and loving God. Be free from restraint externally and internally. Live according to that freedom with the assurance that the God who forgave, justified and reconciled will be faithful in the future as this same God has already been faithful to his Christ.

> Is it God who justifies? Who is to condemn? If he has given us
> his Son is there anything he will deny us (Rom 8:33–34)?

Nothing can shake that confidence. A person can live for faith and die for faith and be free for others because the person is already free for self, which alone brings peace.

> Therefore since we are justified by faith, we have peace with
> God through our Lord Jesus Christ (Rom 8:6).

Peace

Peace in Israel is the best of everything: long life, fertile flocks, abundant harvest, good friends and family, but, above all, being comfortable in the presence of God. People can live serenely because the hostility has been taken away and nothing "will be able to separate us from the love of God which is in Christ Jesus" (Rom 8:39). Turmoil and conflict may whirl about, but the one who lives in faith lives calmly, with a gentle acceptance. Peace has destroyed the alienation between God and his creation and within creation and between and among people. Serenity has once again become the trademark of humankind.

Joy

And so people are joyful. "Rejoice in your hope" (Rom 12:12). The apostle who suffered much lived a life in which he knew and loved joy. God has been good to him in the past; God will be good to him in the future; God will be good to him in the present. There are always reasons to rejoice and enjoy life and celebrate its goodness and have a good time because God has made his decision plain and that decision is good. Who can ever rob the believer of this joy? What God has given God protects and gives in ever-increasing abundance. And so Paul can rise to the heights of poetry as he proclaims the meaning of his faith:

> If God is for us, who is against us? He who did not spare his own Son but gave him up for us all, will he not also give us all things with him? Who shall bring any charge against God's elect? It is God who justifies. Who is to condemn? Is it Christ Jesus who died, yes, who was raised from the dead, who is at the right hand of God, who indeed intercedes for us? Who shall separate us from the love of Christ? Shall tribulation, or distress, or persecution, or famine, or nakedness, or peril, or sword? As it is written, "For thy sake we are being killed all the day long; we are regarded as sheep to be slaughtered."
>
> No, in all these things we are more than conquerors through him who loves us. For I am sure that neither death, nor life, nor angels, nor principalities, nor things present, nor things to come, nor powers, nor height, nor depth, not anything else in all creation will be able to separate us from the love of God in Christ Jesus our Lord (Rom 8:31–38).

STUDY QUESTIONS

1. Why is community so important in Christianity? Can all not just be individual believers?

2. What does faith mean today?

3. "One another" is an important element in Christian thought. How does it fit into a very individualistic world?

4. Equality is important for all. How does this fit the feminist discussion in the church today? Do you think Paul was a chauvinist?

5. How can Paul's teaching on equality be expressed in the church?

6. Christians are not passive in the sight of God. How so, and why not?

7. Joy should characterize all Christians and the church. The celebration of life, the goodness of creation, the assurance of ultimate victory—all add meaning to Christianity. How is this expressed in various aspects of the church?

Chapter 15

JUSTIFICATION

The meaning of justification in Paul continues to cause controversy within Christianity. Four hundred years after the Protestant reformation, some Christians seem to have resolved the conflict that surrounded Martin Luther and the leaders of the Catholic counter-reformation, but most Christians, both Roman Catholic and Protestant, still differ in their understanding. More often than not, just what the word means to most believers does not have a clear foundation in Paul. People seem to have made up their minds on the sense of "blameless conduct" without too much thought.

Someone might say that justification, righteousness (the Greek word is *dikaiosune*), means that people are "all right," or perhaps we can say that because of justification, people can "stand" in the presence of God. However helpful such efforts to explain are, they do not deal with the reason for such a position. Nor do they fully appreciate the role of the individual vis-à-vis God's activity.

Augustine, and Luther after him when he wrote of "justification by faith alone," were right when they emphasized the gratuity of God's gift of grace through faith. The Council of Trent also recognizes that justification comes through faith. Just making this statement does not, however, explain what it means, neither to Paul nor to his audience nor to Augustine nor Luther nor to the fathers of Trent nor to believers today. Certainly several centuries of discussion, often with great animosity, have not settled the problem.

Perhaps the problem lies in the fundamental way in which Paul thinks along with the methods which surround the interpretation of his thought. When the divine power enters into the ordinary course of human events, things will not always fit into neat categories. The matter becomes more confused when we are accustomed to such

> Let no one say to himself: "If it is of faith, how is it freely given? If faith earns it, why is it not rather paid than given?" Let the faithful man not say that because when he says, "I have faith that I may earn justification," he is answered: "What have you that you have not received" (1 Cor 4:7). Therefore since faith asks for and receives justification, "according as God has divided to everyone the measure of faith" (Rom 12:3), no human merit precedes the grace of God, but grace itself merits an increase, and the increase merits perfection, with the will accompanying it, not going before it; following behind it, not pointing out the way (Augustine, *Letters* #186:3:10).

language as "justification" or "the reign of God" or "salvation" or "redemption" or "grace and faith" and use these words as if we understand perfectly well what they mean. Just ask an ordinary Christian and you will quickly discover that few even agree on some of these fundamental aspects of the meaning of Christianity.

The Church and Paul

An additional problem associated with Paul and justification lies in the uneasiness which both he and his teaching cause the church. Even within the New Testament we see an effort to tame Paul in the writings of the pastorals. These letters seem to have been written to bring Paul and his thinking in line with other thought patterns of the

> We are therefore said to be justified by faith because faith is the beginning of human salvation, the foundation and root of all justification, "without which it is impossible to please God" (Heb 11:6) and to come to the fellowship of his sons; and we are therefore said to be justified gratuitously because none of those things that precede justification, whether faith or works, merits the grace of justification. For "if by grace, it is not now by works"; otherwise as the apostle says, "grace is no more grace" (Rom 11:6) (Trent, chapter VIII, #722).

church at the end of the first century. Paul becomes mellow and wise, full of good counsel, acceptable for a developing hierarchical church.

The power of Paul and his unusual doctrine calls into question many of Christianity's pious traditions. The subtle supports which believers use to bolster their self-image as faithful all fall down when Paul and his teaching are taken seriously. The twentieth century church likes to settle into a comfortable Christianity, often as leisure-time activity, with good deeds that will ensure entrance into heaven. Such an approach to God and faith and Jesus just does not like to be disturbed. And Paul disturbs.

Radical Challenge

The reading of Galatians and Romans makes it difficult to ignore the radical challenge of Paul. Christians often avoid Paul. People seem, for example, to have had already decided who God is and who they are and what the church is. Often many people do not necessarily like any one of the above but they are comfortable. Reading Galatians and Romans opens eyes to the tragedy of humanity which all always knew but wanted to avoid. Reading Paul also helps people to accept the possibility of a gracious act of God in Jesus, allowing people to leave that tragedy behind and live freely as graced—all this, not based on pious observance nor on good deeds nor the avoidance of sin, but only through the loving power of God.

Existential Approach

Accepting Paul and his teaching also can bring relief. Traditional Thomistic philosophy and theology, with its particular methodology or approach, has given way to a more contemporary existential and phenomenological approach. The concerns are this world here and now more than the future life. Human conditions and relationships have taken on more importance than a concern about the relationship to God. Take care of the former and the latter will follow. Many may believe in the deepness of reality but must live on the surface which often masks that deepest of reality. This methodology has greatly influenced contemporary Christian theology, bringing as much criticism as acceptance.

I think Paul was an existential phenomenologist. For him the future will take care of itself, and because of what God has already done for humankind, people can live differently now with each other.

They can believe in the future and live most sure of the presence of God in the deepest recesses of the human spirit and in the deepest recesses of all of the created order. But always they must live on the ordinary level of human life with all of its untidiness and even meanness as well as its glories and joys.

While I believe that Augustine and Luther and Trent were right on the centrality of justification by grace through faith, I should also acknowledge that not all scholars will agree with the interpretation given here. How to interpret Paul will continue to intrigue and disturb. For an existential phenomenologist, this interpretation of justification works, and I believe that what follows is in the mainstream of scholarly interpretation at the present time.

Paul and Righteousness

Paul's understanding of the term in Galatians and Romans comes from a sense of legal righteousness. Since the concept comes from the law court, then some people are already accused of acting wrongly, or, in a religious context, people are accused of sinning. Paul does not stop here. For him *all* have sinned. Sin permeates the whole of human existence. Not just the murderer or the rapist or the child abuser, but even the pious little old ladies and little old men who go to church every day and the orthodox Jew who observes every command of the Torah—all are sinners. The hardened criminal and the righteous Roman Catholic, Protestant, Jew and Muslim are all sinners in the sight of God. No wonder people did not like to listen to him and still do not like to hear him in church!

Sinners All

Historically, some have tried to get every good person off the hook by claiming that Paul was opposed to the law because it was too hard. Luke takes this approach when he remarks: "Now why do you make a trial of God by putting a yoke upon the neck of the disciples which neither our fathers nor we have been able to bear" (Acts 15:10)? Paul responded by saying that he was better than most (Phil 3:4–6), and, in Galatians, "I advanced in Judaism beyond many of my own age among my people, so extremely zealous was I for the traditions of my fathers (1:14). No, for Paul even when people observe the law they are sinners.

To be sinners means to be helpless (Rom 5:1) and enemies of God

(Rom 5:10). Justification brings about a reconciliation, but not of God being reconciled to people but rather of people being reconciled to God. Such is strange, since it almost seems that humankind becomes the offended party and humanity needs to be reconciled to God (2 Cor 5:20). If nothing more, Paul has an unusual understanding of sin. Instead of sin being something people do against God, sin is rather the attempt to establish one's own justification, to understand human life as a project to be accomplished, a prize to be won, an existence to be secured. Actually, to sin is to play God and tell God, "You owe me because of how I lived, so now give me eternal life!"

Performance

On the level of consciousness, by attempting to fulfill life's project, believers try to lessen the anxiety about the future. But all know that the anxiety never goes away. For the people who worry the most, the anxiety gets stronger, so that all is directed toward the fulfillment of one's life project. Then the person can tell God: "You owe me."

Paul has uncovered a fundamental human condition. People do things because they want others to respond and tell them that they are good people. "I want my place in the sun in the eyes of others. I want to be known as good and kind and generous, dedicated, dependable, straight arrow, nice person to be with and have around." All these are part of life's project, and by doing certain things and avoiding others, everyone can complete the project and have the place in the sun here and then in the life to come. All this Paul attacks. Again, no wonder people did not like him and the official church tried to tame him. The performance principle rules and lives within the church as well as in the marketplace.

The law had promised release from sin and instead brought death. In Romans 9:30, Paul refers to the righteous law because the law demands righteousness. Paul saw the law as a condition for righteousness, but this period in the history of salvation has now passed with the coming of Christ. The law could not really bring righteousness and thus the law no longer can be a means of righteousness. In Galatians 3:21 Paul explicitly denies that righteousness can come from the law. Paul must clarify his understanding of righteousness in light of his previous thinking. Somehow the Pharisees must understand his commitment to Christ and his previous commitment to the law. A new relationship has become possible not through the law. Paul takes over a sacred Jewish idea when he writes of righteousness, but then turns it against any legal concept. Fulfillment of the law will not bring justification.

Traditionally, Jews, and most Christians, view God as a judge who rewards the good and punishes the bad. Both Jews and Christians also subscribe to the notion of a sinful humanity as depicted in the early chapters of Genesis. If people are to enjoy a favorable relationship with God, if they are to be justified and righteous, then they must obey God and all of the commandments. This results in righteousness and reward. Paul, however, parts company with such ideas, for, in Christ, God alone established fellowship or friendship or righteousness with humanity. People do not accomplish this on their own through their good works. God intervened sovereignly and freely and graciously in Jesus. This alone established the proper relationship with the human race, and not all of the good works of the law in the history of humankind. The movement has passed from humanity to God, since alone humankind lives in a sinful existence. Even when people attempt to live according to the law, they commit the greatest sin by thinking they can control God and cash in their chips when they die.

The Righteousness of God

Salvation, the actual experience of God bringing well-being and fulfillment and contentment, depends on the individual being justified or righteous. Whenever Paul writes of this salvation, he speaks of it as accomplished by the righteousness of God. No doubt exists in his mind: God alone justifies and God alone brings the individual to a level of acceptance and love and understanding. Judgment involves grace imparting a pardoning sentence. The accused is acquitted, declared innocent, bringing the reign of God as new life. This reign begun now will be completed on the last day in the final judgment of grace: "Who shall bring any charge against God's elect? It is God who justifies; who is to condemn?" (Rom 8:33–34).

The final eschatological judgment has already taken place in the death of Jesus (Rom 3:21–26; 5:1, 9). The judgment is acquittal for all (Rom 5:18). God has universally acquitted sinful people. The impious are justified (Rom 4:5) as a pure gift of God. God has given persons life without demanding any payment of good deeds.

In Romans, Paul clearly extends this righteousness to all, Jew and Gentile. Righteousness goes beyond the acceptance of the individual by God, extending it to the human race. God does not pick and choose

---

SALVATION

- actual experience of God now
- well-being and contentment
- happiness and fulfillment
- acceptance and love and understanding
- grace pardoning now
- acquittal, innocent, new life now

---

those whom God would like to justify, but rather the love of God in freedom and grace covers humanity. To use an analogy by Luther in a slightly different way, this grace falls upon humanity much as the snow falls upon hill and dale, covering ground, grass and plants. Nothing fails to feel its effect. The universal divine gift of grace took place in Christ Jesus, and all of humanity has been affected and is graced.

Imagine! Such a thought allows the greatest monsters that humanity has produced to be justified. What of the virtuous, those who do all for God, those who live piously, the true ethical heroes? But no one can stand before God with piety in hand. No one can boast in the presence of God. Everyone stands alone and naked before the God who graciously gives. Thus teaches Paul.

God's Power

Making righteous the human race manifests God's power. If God could render judgment in wrath and punishment—and the biblical tradition is filled with examples of this power—so God can also exercise power in bringing his saving presence. In Romans 1:18, Paul makes reference of the wrath of God. Now the wrath with its great power gives way to reconciliation. Once wrath had been revealed, but now righteousness in grace takes its place.

All the activity of God's power in justifying takes place on the cross (Rom 3:25; 5:9 Gal 3:13). We usually think of the resurrection as accomplishing human salvation, but Paul will never separate the exaltation of Jesus from his crucifixion. God declaring justice is not an abstract decree in the heavenly realm. The righteousness of the human race takes place historically in the death of Jesus. God raised up the crucified Jesus as justified, as holy and blameless. Humanity had set out to destroy the goodness that was Jesus, but God would declare Jesus righteous in his resurrection. In so doing, people could experience a similar declaration of justification.

Certainly, righteousness belongs properly to God. In God, justice and grace become united as one. Unlike Judaism, which strove in vain to unite the goodness of God to justice, in Paul God unites both in Jesus on the cross. Forgiveness becomes a judgment by God in which justice is also vindicated. God declares that evil cannot have power over his righteousness in Christ Jesus.

God declares the believer to be righteous, but this is no mere forensic declaration without foundation in fact. The sovereign sentence of God becomes effective. It does not mean that moral rectitude has been achieved but rather that the individual so declared is "right" in the presence of God because God has so declared. All that God declares becomes reality. This justification of the unjust goes beyond all human standards. Grace burst the forms of previous thought patterns and leaves the individual in a position of profound acceptance of a gift. The idea of rewards and punishments, balance sheets and debits gives way to an understanding of justice on the divine plane. All human categories lie shattered at the foot of the cross. Paul presents an understanding of justification as a paradox. The divine judge remains so through the declaration and actual accomplishment of a specific sentence. The individual may stand in the presence of God as "right."

Individual Faith

We might tend to view this sense of righteousness as forgiveness, and Paul does include this idea but goes beyond it. God not only forgives but saves, helps and brings about a reconciliation and deliverance. People are truly different. The great gift is both given and received (Rom 5:17; 8:10). Because the righteousness is both given and received, this quality will determine the life of the believer. The righteous God has brought about a change in the life of the individual. God constantly imparts the gift of grace in righteousness, not because of anything that the person has done but as pure gift. The gift takes up the individual into the very righteousness of God and makes the person righteous and justified and saved because of this one righteousness of God. The person accepts in faith.

Faith alone draws the person into salvation and righteousness. For Paul, people are justified and become righteous when they respond in faith to the presence of God in Jesus and are baptized and receive his Spirit (Gal 3:6; 1:5). The individual must submit to the righteousness of God (Rom 10:3). Faith is the condition: "He who through faith is righteous shall live" (Rom 1:17). The actual achievement and declaration of salvation in righteousness is always linked to the appropriation of salvation because a personal relationship must exist between God and the individual. The foundation for all on the part of the individual remains faith and faith alone. In Romans 3:21, Paul explicitly refers to righteousness through faith. Faith, however, is not a good work but rather a divine gift. The individual accepts the offer made by God in a suppliant way, paying no attention to personal merit and with no concern for reward or punishment.

Hope, the Spirit and Holiness

Justification also demands hope. Present salvation will give way to future salvation when all will be accomplished in God. In Judaism the question of salvation must wait until the final judgment. In Christianity, the future is assured now. Believers can await a future with confidence. The justified who have been grasped by the divine power in the cross can look forward with confidence to the final declaration for the human race. In the act of justification, God has begun the total renewal of humanity which will certainly be brought to a completion (Rom 8:3).

Justification brings a power for new life to the individual who believes. The believer becomes drawn into the reign of God now and is moved toward a future which brings a renewal of all life. Sin is a movement to death; justification is a movement to life. For Paul all is accomplished through the power of the Spirit. Through the spirit the individual lives a life of service not based on merit but flowing from the reality that God has affected within. Righteousness overcomes sin, bringing the believer to the living power in the spirit to live a life based on righteousness. Thus the believer is holy. Right action flows from righteousness. The justifying sentence of God leads to a righteous state of the new life.

The great gift of God to the individual, accepted in faith, overcomes sin and makes the individual graced and holy. With a sense of hope in a complete experience of God, the individual lives his or her life in service. The Spirit has been given and transforms the individual to a new way of living, effecting righteous actions, flowing from the righteousness in the person. Moral rectitude is not yet attained, but the righteous person can stand in the presence of God. The believer is "right" with God because God has so constituted the one who believes and accepts the great gift.

Deliverance

Much of how a person thinks of life or self or church or relationships depends on how the person thinks of himself or herself in the sight of God. If things are all right with God, then things will be all right on earth with others. If an individual constantly thinks that righteousness with God depends on good deeds, then the presence of bad deeds can only cause dejection, depression and sadness. If a person can believe in the ability to stand in God's presence not because of self, but because of God, then life can be happy. Life can take on new meaning and bring peace even in the presence of human failure. Who we are will depend on what we have become in faith.

Paul felt delivered from the burden of a law he could never fulfill, although he had given himself to such a task. The emphasis moved from Paul to God in Christ, and Paul experienced a sense of deliverance. Now he had an enthusiasm for life which knew no bounds. No wonder he was disappointed when the Galatians decided to return to an understanding of salvation and righteousness based on law and the performance of good works. Paul had tried that path and had failed. Now he could boast in God and not self, and that alone brought him salvation and righteousness and grace and peace.

Centuries later, Christians still debate the relationship between faith and good works. Believers still think in terms of rewards and punishments and the appearance before the divine tribunal in death. Paul wanted to shift the emphasis from humanity to God but humanity finds it hard to accept such a shift. Surely such a teaching does not mean that people can just go and sin and not worry about it. Paul explicitly condemns this. But he does seem to imply that people should not be worried over failure and sin. Such concerns do little to help anyone. Concentrate rather on the greatness of God and then failure and sin become relative. If God loved all in their sins and justified all when still sinners, how much more does God care for people now!

Peace eludes the human race too often, for most people fail to look for peace in the right place. God has declared his sentence on humanity, and his sentence is effective. God's word goes forth and accomplishes its task (Is 55:11). The judgment is good. People, all people, are meant to be right with God, meant to stand in the presence of God with dignity—not due to all of the good works accomplished in the history of humankind but only because of a God who had so established the righteousness of humanity through the cross and resurrection of Jesus his Son. The future has to be good, for the future rests upon a past in which the saving presence of God has entered into human history, in the life, death and resurrection of one who is like us in all things but sin. This Jesus welcomes the acceptance of freely given grace in faith. That alone is necessary. Thus believed Paul, the apostle to the Gentiles. Thus preached Paul and continues to teach through his writings, especially the epistles to the Galatians and the Romans.

STUDY QUESTIONS

1. What does justification mean to you?

2. How do works fit in with a loving and saving God?

3. Is everyone really saved? Does it make any difference whether you are Jew or Christian, Catholic or Protestant or Orthodox?

4. How should the meaning of justification affect church structure?

5. Has Paul's teaching become ingrained in Christianity? Has it been forgotten?

6. How would you explain justification to a family member, a friend, a child?

7. Has the debate on justification between Catholics and Protestants in the reformation period ever been concluded?

8. What really matters in a person's life if God justifies?

9. What is your image of God after Galatians and Romans and the study of justification? Do you like the image?

Chapter 16

PAUL'S MANY IMAGES OF JESUS

Paul understands Jesus not in some theoretical way but as a vital dynamic component of his life, directed toward living the Christian life, a result of personal experience and the living of the apostolic life. Founded on his personal experience of the risen Lord, this appreciation of the meaning of Jesus has also been influenced by tradition. Reading the various letters of Paul, the student can detect a development in Paul's christology. Above all, he sees Jesus as savior; God has communicated and offered himself through Jesus and unites and reconciles people and the world through this same savior. The titles used by Paul when referring to Jesus express the function of the coming of Christ for Paul and manifest both the salvation dimension of Jesus and the relationship of Jesus to God as his Father. Galatians and Romans do not offer a complete picture of Pauline christology. They do give us some general insights into the thought of Paul on Jesus. A study of other letters added to Galatians and Romans will help fill out the picture.

The Jesus of Personal Experience

Paul recognized the speaker who introduced himself on the road to Damascus as "Jesus, whom you are persecuting," as the exalted Son of God. This Lord, however, was for Paul the same as the historical Jesus of Nazareth who had been crucified some three years previously. Paul did not know this historical Jesus, and so his perspective would of necessity differ from that of the twelve apostles or those earliest followers of Jesus.

Nevertheless, Paul first tells us about this historical Jesus of Nazareth, since his letters are the first literary expressions of Christianity. Jesus was a descendant of Abraham (Gal 3:16) and David (Rom 1:3), lived under the law (Gal 4:4), endured crucifixion (Gal 3:1), and was experienced as risen by Paul himself (Gal 1:16).

Paul also knew Peter, James and John (Gal 1:19; 2:9), and although he does not quote actual words of Jesus, he seems to be well acquainted with the substance of his teachings. We have only to compare the ethical section of Romans (12–15) with the sermon on the mount to discover the close relationship between what Matthew presents as a way of living for believers and what Paul offers. What Paul says of the life and teaching of the historical Jesus fits well with the understanding of this same historical person as recorded in the gospels.

We should realize, however, that some of the most familiar aspects of the historical Jesus that we learn of in the gospels we have no record of in Paul. In the gospels Jesus habitually teaches in parables, heals the sick, drives out demons. None of this appears in the letters of Paul. Nor would we know of the controversies faced by Jesus and the events that led up to his death if we only had the testimony of Paul. The christology of Paul agrees with that of the evangelists and differs.

Some have tried to develop the christology of Paul from Gnosticism, Hellenistic philosophy and a refined sense of Judaism. But Paul knew Jesus as risen Lord and understood the meaning of God's anointed not from a mixture of Gnosticism and Hellenism and Judaism, but from personal contact. Often in the past scholars have tried to detect foreign influences in Paul and his theology. Surely he could not live in a pluralistic world without feeling some of its effects. We have already admitted that. His portrait of Jesus, however, comes from personal contact. His christology does not consist of some abstract doctrine but finds its foundation in the historical Jesus of Nazareth who died, whom he persecuted and who appeared to him on the road to Damascus. But now this same Jesus sits at the right hand of God and becomes the center of Paul's personal religion.

According to Paul, Jesus had been designated Son of God in power according to the Spirit of holiness by the resurrection from the dead (Rom 1:4). The emphasis falls on God as the agent who made Jesus Son of God in power because he had already been endowed with the spirit of holiness. As a result, God raised Jesus from the dead. This same divine power works now among the followers of Jesus, conveyed to them through the indwelling Spirit. The christology of Paul also involves the continuing presence of the Spirit in believers which attests to the final consummation when all, Jew and Greek, will experience the fullness of salvation in the resurrection of the dead.

Jesus and Paul's Personality

While all of his christology results from personal experience, we also must take into consideration Paul's temperament. Paul the Pharisee tried to fulfill all of the law but labored under an internal conflict, since he realized that he could never fulfill such law (Rom 7:7). In Jesus, Paul recognized a redeemer who brought the salvation of God, the saving presence of God, and gave grace freely. The convert Paul lived supremely conscious of the once fractured life that was made whole by the grace of God in Christ Jesus.

Glorified Christ

Paul's personal Christ was the glorified Jesus, living eternally in his definitive state as resurrected Lord and Christ. This same Jesus is also the mystical Christ united by reason of identity with his followers whom Paul had persecuted. People experience salvation by accepting the offer of the communication of the glorious life of Jesus (Gal 2:20), and Paul as an apostle proclaims this to Jew and Gentile alike.

Paul always related the Christ of the Spirit to the Jesus of the flesh in history (2 Cor 5:16), including in his personal understanding the pre-existing and transcendent Christ. All that Paul understood in his christology came from this personal experience, which was mystical and existential. In some ways this understanding of Jesus went beyond that of the twelve, for Paul started from the glorious Christ, affirmed his earthly existence, and then, finally, preached some type of pre-existence which culminates his christology in the fullness of the life of the risen and glorious Christ with God his Father.

Paul Receives from Tradition

Paul based his christology on personal experience (Gal 1:12), but also clearly acknowledged his dependence upon the traditions of the early communities (1 Cor 15:3–5). He preached a risen Lord with a history received from tradition from the early church. He writes of the historical Jesus: "born of a woman, born under the law" (Gal 4:4); the seed of David (Rom 1:3); "crucified" (Gal 3:1). This same Jesus

instituted the eucharist the night before he was betrayed (1 Cor
11:23); he suffered (Rom 15:3) and was obedient unto death (2 Cor
1:5; Phil 3:10). Paul even records certain sayings of the historical
Jesus (1 Cor 7:10; 9:14; Rom 14:4; 1 Thes 4:14). Paul continued the
preaching of Jesus, especially the coming of the kingdom, the pri-
macy of love, and the apostles as servants of all.

The combination of personal experience and the tradition of the
early church flowed into each other to create a multifaceted portrait
of Jesus that ebbed and rose, responding to the various needs of Paul
and his listeners.

The Progression of Paul's Christology

Development characterizes human life. Surely a growth in awareness and understanding would characterize the church's understanding of Jesus. The same remains true for all believers, especially evi-
denced in Paul.

The early Paul (1 Thessalonians and 1 Corinthians) emphasized
the second coming of Jesus. This christology seems close to that of
Acts but with further development. Jesus as Lord occupies the central
place, equal to the Father. The resurrection of Jesus constitutes the
first moment and prelude of the final act, which will be the second
and glorious coming. With the risen Lord people can be sanctified.
Salvation and the kingdom are no longer just future realities, but
present *now*. At this period of Paul's thought, the actual coming of
Jesus into history has little importance. The incarnate Word of God in
Jesus of Nazareth gives way to the glorious and risen Lord and Christ.
Paul differs from the gospels, for example, which often see the ministry of Jesus as one continuous epiphany of God in Jesus.

In 2 Corinthians, Galatians and Romans, Paul emphasizes Jesus as
the one who brings salvation. The law cannot justify people; only faith
in Christ Jesus can bring the saving presence of God's grace. This
offer Paul proclaims to all. Law gives way to faith; the Jew receives
the offer as does the Gentile; the church becomes the new people of
God. All of this Paul preaches in 2 Corinthians 5:18–19.

In Philippians and Ephesians (whether Paul wrote this or not
remains disputed as we have noted), some of the controversies seem
to have subsided. Faith has overcome the law and Gentiles are freely
welcomed into the community. Now Paul concentrates on the mystery of Jesus the Christ, prepared for in the wisdom of God before the
foundations of the world. His meaning had been announced in the

scriptures and effected and completed in the Christ who lives now with full majesty and glory at the right hand of God. The cosmic Christ, the transcendent savior, reigns eternally.

Philippians expressed the personal Christ who is savior and Lord of all (Phil 3:20), but this same Christ had emptied himself (Phil 2). The pre-existent Christ becomes the center of all and the consummation of the universe. With an emphasis on dignity the letter to the Ephesians explained the Christ by attributes of wisdom and focused on the saving power; God chose us according to his good pleasure; by the super liberality of God we share in the riches of the divine and we are all predestined in Christ (Eph 1:3–14).

The Hymn in Philippians 2:6–11

Perhaps no greater expression of Pauline christology can be found than that of the hymn in the second chapter of Philippians. In the past some have claimed that Paul actually composed the hymn; others, by far the majority, believe that Paul found the hymn already existing and incorporated it into his letter, adding some additional elements to suit his purpose. To understand the hymn demands an appreciation of its context both in the epistle and in the influence of the Philippian community in the life of Paul.

Paul loved the Philippians more than any other community he founded. His personal attitude toward this group of believers becomes evident in the reading of the epistle. Everything written in this letter should be seen not as a missionary document, nor as an effort to correct problems, but rather that this favorite community might grow in the knowledge and love of their faith in Christ Jesus.

Paul viewed the Christians at Philippi differently from other communities. He wanted them to more fully understand and live the life of Jesus in their personal lives, and in this epistle he used hymns more so than in any other letter. For Paul this group of early believers had already reached a level of understanding that demanded him to encourage them to continue to imitate the living Christ. Paul loved this community and anxiously led them to ever greater understanding and love of their faith in the Lord Jesus. With this as background, we can better understand the hymn and what Paul hoped to accomplish in his writing.

Have this mind among yourselves, which you have in Christ Jesus, who though he was in the form of God did not think this equality was something to be proudly paraded, but emptied himself, taking the form of a servant, being born in the likeness of men. And being found in human form he humbled himself and became obedient to death, even to death on the cross. Therefore God has exalted him and bestowed on him the name that is above every name, that at the name of Jesus every knee should bend in heaven and on earth and under the earth, and every tongue should confess that Jesus Christ is Lord, to the glory of God the Father (Phil 2:5–11).

Paul offered a full christological presentation with elements involving the person of Jesus, his ministry moving from pre-existence to the consummation of the world. In this hymn Paul presents three specific phases:

- *pre-mundane (pre-existence)*, the historical phase and eschatological phase: pre-existence: he was in the form of God but entered into human history as a servant.
- *earthly life*: servanthood led him to death on a cross in obedience to God.
- *exaltation*: God glorifies Jesus in his resurrection and makes it possible for all to overcome death and share in the same glorification. The exalted Jesus is now Lord of the universe and all, even adverse powers, must acknowledge him as such.

To understand the idea of "the form of God" demands a comparison with "servant form." Paul presents Jesus as being equal to God, sharing in the glory of God but also distinct from God since God exalted Christ. This form is not to be proudly paraded. He never explains the equality. Surely he does not mean divine essence, for then we would never understand an "emptying." The form of God is not the essence of God, just as the form of a servant is not the essence of being human. He who did not have the form of a servant accepted it without losing the form of God. He (Paul does not name the "he") accepts not just human nature but the sinful humanity. As obedient servant, Jesus goes to the cross and as a result God gives him the name above all names. In the biblical tradition, a name expressed the essence or meaning of a person. God enthrones Jesus as *Lord*, and all must now acknowledge him as such.

The hymn is not a complete theological treatise on christology. Rather, as a poem, the hymn expresses some understanding of Jesus by one who loved ardently and wrote poetically. Paul found the hymn and sent it on to the Philippians who could meditate on its meaning and acknowledge that their savior Jesus was the exalted Lord of all. They could turn to him in worship and receive his comforting grace.

Pauline Christology in General

The personal christology of Paul did not concentrate on the earthly life of Jesus. For Paul, that Jesus lives was sufficient. But now he was risen and existed as glorious savior and Lord of all. The early preachers and evangelists paid more attention to the life and ministry of Jesus and showed the identity between the man who suffered and died on the cross and the one who was raised from the dead. Paul concentrated on the life of the glorious Lord living now with God and in his church. The man Jesus came from the Jews but was destined to save all people by dying and being raised by God.

Crucified Messiah

Jesus was true messiah, but also crucified messiah. The crucified Jesus forms the foundation for Paul's preaching. We have seen this in Galatians and Romans. Salvation by the law gives way to salvation by faith in the cross of Jesus. Thus we have the scandal of the cross (1 Cor 2:2; Gal 5:11; 6:12). Paul, however, will not remain on the level of the earthly death of Jesus. Faith in the cross of Jesus takes its strength from faith in the resurrected Lord (Rom 4:14). Cross and resurrection are constituted as one in the mind of Paul, which is expressed in his formula:

who was put to death for our trespasses and raised for our justification (Rom 4:25).

Both cross and resurrection need to be personally accepted by the Christian. In Romans, Paul sees this in baptism (Rom 6:3). The cross is the place of the expiatory death for all (Gal 3:13) and the resurrection is the giving of new life, made so by the Spirit (Rom 8:9–11). Only through Jesus as Christ can we ever understand human existence. Cross and resurrection will constitute the life of the believer just as it constituted the life of Jesus.

Titles of Jesus

Son: Paul used this title sixteen times and in diverse meanings and contexts. The pre-existent Son: Rom 8:3; Gal 4:4. Crucified Son: Rom

5:10; 8:32. In Romans 1:3–4, we find an ancient formula used by Paul which we have already seen: Son of David and Son of God in power. In Romans 8:3, what was impossible by law becomes possible in the coming of the Son in sinful flesh. Such a Son accepts a salvific office and is able to restore a sinful world. In Romans 8:32, God did not spare his own Son but gave him up for us. The love of God for the Son and vice versa and the love of God and Son for humankind form the reasons for the salvation of all. In Romans 8:8–11, the Son of God makes others share in this relationship. The same idea is present in Galatians 4:1–7. Christ as God's Son sends his Spirit to make us adopted children of God. God himself had revealed his Son to Paul on the road to Damascus (Gal 1:16), and now Paul proclaims that all can relate to God as did Jesus.

Lord: The title carries with it a sense of adoration. Paul accepted the title from the Christian community and gave it a proper character. In Romans 14:9, we see it in relationship to reigning. In the Old Testament it refers to God, and Paul used it forty-seven times either alone or in conjunction with Christ. The exalted Lord will come again and demand adoration. This same Lord accepted his death (Rom 14:8).

Christ: Jesus is the messiah, the anointed one, the chosen one who will bring salvation to all. God had sent Jesus to live a human life in obedience unto death. Then, as chosen anointed one, Jesus the Christ became the Lord of all, offering salvation to all, Jew and Gentile.

Paul allowed his understanding of Jesus his Lord and Christ to unfold as his life unfolded. He never developed a complete christology since such would be possible for Paul only when he himself had completed his journey. He gives to every Christian community starting points, for ultimately Paul believes that christology, the understanding of love of Jesus the Lord, is personal. Such it was for him. So it shall be for all.

STUDY QUESTIONS

1. Why are there so many images of Jesus in the New Testament? Does the existence of a development in christology help faith or hinder it?

2. The Jesus of personal experience seems fundamental. Is this true for everyone's life?

3. Is Jesus a Jew for Paul? Why is he more than a Jew?

4. Paul has his religious experience of Jesus and then continues to develop in his understanding of Jesus. Why is such a journey helpful for a spiritual life?

5. The hymn in Philippians seems exotic. Does it make sense? What are the implications for systematic christology, for a personal relationship with Jesus?

6. The crucified Jesus remains central for Paul and for Christianity. How is this present in the contemporary church? In the contemporary Christian?

7. Do the various titles of Jesus used by Paul add much in understanding?

8. Do you like the Jesus of Paul?

9. Develop your own progression of Pauline christology. What elements are fundamental and which flow from these foundations?

CONCLUSION

Chapter 17

PAUL'S GOSPEL TODAY

After almost two thousand years of Christianity the gospel of the Lord Jesus still challenges, as does Paul. Years tend to obscure. The baggage of centuries can overwhelm and the dust of history lessen the sharpness of the unusual gospel of Jesus. Paul has shared in this obscurity. Both Jesus and Paul, however, still stir the uneasiness within the human spirit.

Almost regularly through the centuries, Christians will turn to Paul and once again "discover" his understanding of the Jesus tradition, only to find him lost in the next wave. Augustine turned to Romans when Roman civilization crumbled. Luther and Calvin learned from Romans as they ignited the Protestant reformation. In this century Karl Barth trumpeted the return of the transcendent God and the demise of liberal Protestantism with his commentary on Romans. Paul always manages to stand in the middle of any attempt to renew Christianity.

Roman Catholics historically have not been as interested in Paul, and in particular Galatians and Romans, as Protestants have. Historically the Roman Catholic Church has followed the guidelines of Matthew or Luke. When the official church expressed an interest in Paul, it turned rather to the non-authentic Pauline letters called the pastorals.

Whether Catholic or Protestant, however, all contemporary believers can learn much from Paul, and in particular from these two great pillars of his gospel, Galatians and Romans. The thought of the apostle to the Gentiles stands as a clarion calling to pay attention to the root of belief. His gospel shines like a beacon, pointing out with clarity some of the fundamental aspects of the meaning of Jesus. Paul and his gospel live with a vitality that can always renew.

Certain characteristics of Paul's gospel need to be lifted up and cherished. In a world that depends too much on self, people would gain much by depending more on God. In a society which judges people on productivity and merit, all folk, common or not, should feel good if they can believe that God loves them for themselves.

Any writer who tries to sum up the thought of Paul does so with hesitation. How can one pick out the most important elements of the thought of someone who so shaped much of the New Testament? Choosing those aspects of his doctrine which are particularly helpful today is the excuse which settles the mind. Such a decision leaves out the impossible challenge to summarize all of Paul's thought.

The Goodness of God

Anyone who reads Galatians and Romans knows Paul's strong conviction of the goodness of God. God has loved humanity in its sinfulness. God has offered salvation, the experience of a comforting presence. God has offered redemption: the assurance that goodness will never be destroyed. Paul would join in with enthusiasm and sing to God: "How great thou art!" God has given us Jesus. Therefore, God will deny us nothing. "How good is God!"

The Universality of God's Goodness

God plays no favorites. No longer does one group have the edge. Jews and Gentiles belong. That leaves no one out. Historically, religions tend to be exclusive. Paul says: No! God invites all, for God has already predestined all to live forever. Jesus the Christ has made salvation possible for all and not just for a few, or for the best, or the pious, or the bright, or the rich, or the poor, or the saint, or the sinner. God has declared humanity blessed and saved and redeemed.

The Dignity and Worth of Everyone

What a person means does not depend on what a person does. Productivity and merit mean nothing in the eyes of God. The goodness of the person is a gift, given at birth, and no one can take that away, not even the individual person. Worthiness depends on what God has given and not on what someone accomplishes. God loves sinners in their sins and so sinners can love themselves. The dirt and grime of history and society may obscure the value of the person, but God sees through the externals and loves that which lives underneath.

The Future Is Good

Too often, people tend to think of the future as a repetition of the past. God has said no in Christ. The future, not only for humanity but for all creation, is good. Together, the human race and its world are rushing forward to revel in the freedom of the children of God. Creation itself anxiously awaits the full revelation of the destruction of evil and sin. Then humankind and the glory of this world will together reflect the goodness of the one creator of all.

Sin Is Relativized

All are sinners and all deserve the wrath of God, Jew and Gentile. Paul knows that. Paul also knows that sin has not turned God away from humankind. God calls people to live according to the Spirit. God wants people to love each other and care for each other. Paul knows the meaning of the love of God and also knows the failure of humanity, both personal and collective. People will continue to sin as they await the fullness of salvation. Paul does not encourage sin but rather encourages continuing to live according to the Spirit even when people do sin. If everyone sins and God still loves humanity in spite of that sin, then when a person actually fails, colloquially, "No big deal!" "Get up and try again!" God still loves.

Depend Upon God

Perhaps more than any other aspect of Paul's teaching, people have to depend on God. Depending on oneself leaves very little room for anything. Depending on God has limitless possibilities. Left on its own, the human race has not fared well. Being left on one's own only brings personal disaster. Depending on God with the confidence of a young child in the presence of a loving parent brings security and comfort and the realization of the great human potential. Left on their own, people die every time they hurt. Dependence upon God brings ever-renewed life springing up to eternal life.

The Blessedness of the Lord Jesus Christ

How could anyone say anything about Paul's theology without commenting on the centrality of the Lord? Paul had experienced the Lord on the road to Damascus. His life changed. He met a compassionate and forgiving savior. He encountered a suffering messiah, risen in power. He followed a supportive Lord who invited Paul to share in his death and so share in his resurrection.

Paul knew the Lord. Paul wanted to be with the Lord. Paul did what the Lord asked. Jesus and Paul shared a common life in the Spirit. Christ lived in him and he lived in Christ. That explains his apostleship, his writings, his history. Jesus the Christ accepted Paul as he was: the religious personality, the fiery temperament, the impatient crusader, the masterful builder, the eloquent preacher, the compelling writer, the humbled believer, the crushed apostle, the weakened follower. Paul believed in and loved the Lord Jesus, and that was enough.

Some may choose other pillars of Paul's gospel rather than Galatians and Romans. Corinthians comes immediately to mind. Some may also think that Philippians offers an additional pillar. Maybe Paul's gospel has many pillars. No matter what position someone may take on the real and complete Paul, no one can overlook Galatians and Romans. They are at least *two* of the pillars of Paul's gospel, and in this writer's mind they are the foundation pillars. How noble they stand!

STUDY QUESTIONS

1. Does Paul's understanding of the Jesus tradition help the contemporary Christian? Why is it always needed in the church?

2. Does Paul's understanding of Jesus and God help people in their own understanding of God and themselves?

3. Paul could write eloquently of the future. How can this sure hope be incorporated into daily Christian living?

4. Galatians and Romans are pillars of Paul's thought. After a study of these two great works, how have they affected your thinking, praying, confidence, image of God, image of self? Do they help in making life worth living?

5. What does it all mean, this teaching of Paul?

FOR FURTHER READING

Chapter 1. The Apostle Paul and His Background

Buckley, Thomas. *Apostle to the Nations*. Boston: St. Paul, 1980.
Fitzmyer, Joseph A., S.J. *Paul and His Theology*. Englewood Cliffs, NJ: Prentice Hall, 1987, 27–30.

Chapter 2. Paul's Religious Experience

Fitzmyer, Joseph A., S.J. *Paul and His Theology*. Englewood Cliffs, NJ: Prentice Hall, 1987.
James, William. *The Varieties of Religious Experience*. New York: Random House, 1929.
Otto, Rudolph. *The Idea of the Holy*. New York: Oxford University Press, 1958.
Stanley, David. "Paul's Conversion in Acts," *The Catholic Biblical Quarterly*, Vol. 15 (1953), 315–338.

Chapter 3. Paul and Jerusalem

Achtemeier, Paul J. *The Quest for Unity in the New Testament Church*. Philadelphia: Fortress, 1987.
Brown, Raymond E. and Meier, John P. *Antioch and Rome*. New York: Paulist Press, 1983.

Chapter 4. Paul's Gospel

Fitzmyer, Joseph A., S.J. *Paul and His Theology.* Englewood Cliffs, NJ: Prentice Hall, 1987.
Keck, Leander. *Paul and His Letters.* Philadelphia, Fortress, 1979.

Chapter 5. Introduction to Galatians

Cousar, Charles. *Galatians.* Atlanta: John Knox, 1982.

Chapter 6. Paul and His Gospel

Betz, Hans Dieter. *Galatians.* Philadelphia: Fortress, 1979.
Cousar, Charles. *Galatians.* Atlanta: John Knox, 1982.
Osiek, Carolyn. *Galatians.* Wilmington: Glazier, 1982.

Chapter 7. Salvation by Faith

Betz, Hans Dieter. *Galatians.* Philadelphia: Fortress, 1979.
Cousar, Charles. *Galatians.* Atlanta: John Knox, 1982.

Chapter 8. Freedom, the Spirit and the Christian Life

Betz, Hans Dieter. *Galatians.* Philadelphia: Fortress, 1979.
Cousar, Charles. *Galatians.* Atlanta: John Knox, 1982.
Osiek, Carolyn. *Galatians.* Wilmington: Glazier, 1982.

Chapter 9. Introduction to Romans

Achtemeier, Paul J. *Romans.* Atlanta: John Knox, 1985.
Barth, Karl. *The Epistle to the Romans.* London: Oxford University Press, 1950.
Donfried, Karl, ed. *The Romans Debate.* Minneapolis: Augsburg, 1977.
Heil, John P. *Paul's Letter to the Romans.* New York: Paulist Press, 1987.
Käsemann, Ernst. *Commentary on Romans.* Grand Rapids: Eerdmans, 1980.
Maly, Eugene. *Romans.* Wilmington: Glazier, 1979.

Wedderburn, A.J.M. *The Reason for Romans.* Minneapolis: Fortress, 1991.
Ziesler, John. *Paul's Letter to the Romans.* London: SCM, 1989.

Chapter 10. Universal Sin

Achtemeier, Paul J. *Romans.* Atlanta: John Knox, 1985.
Barth, Karl. *The Epistle to the Romans.* London: Oxford University Press, 1950.

Chapter 11. The Gospel of Faith

Achtemeier, Paul J. *Romans.* Atlanta: John Knox, 1985.
Barth, Karl. *The Epistle to the Romans.* London: Oxford University Press, 1950.
Heil, John P. *Paul's Letter to the Romans.* New York: Paulist Press, 1987.
Käsemann, Ernst. *Commentary on Romans.* Grand Rapids: Eerdmans, 1980.

Chapter 12. Israel, Christianity and God's Grace

Achtemeier, Paul J. *Romans.* Atlanta: John Knox, 1985.
Barth, Karl. *The Epistle to the Romans.* London: Oxford University Press, 1950.
Heil, John P. *Paul's Letter to the Romans.* New York: Paulist Press, 1987.
Käsemann, Ernst. *Commentary on Romans.* Grand Rapids: Eerdmans, 1980.
Maly, Eugene. *Romans.* Wilmington: Glazier, 1979.

Chapter 13. The Living of Graced Believers

Achtemeier, Paul J. *Romans.* Atlanta: John Knox, 1985.
Barth, Karl. *The Epistle to the Romans.* London: Oxford University Press, 1950.
Donfried, Karl, ed. *The Romans Debate.* Minneapolis: Augsburg, 1977.

Heil, John P. *Paul's Letter to the Romans.* New York: Paulist Press, 1987.

Käsemann, Ernst. *Commentary on Romans.* Grand Rapids: Eerdmans, 1980.

Maly, Eugene. *Romans.* Wilmington: Glazier, 1979.

Wedderburn, A.J.M. *The Reason for Romans.* Minneapolis, Fortress, 1991.

Ziesler, John. *Paul's Letter to the Romans.* London: SCM, 1989.

Chapter 14. The New Community of Faith

Fitzmyer, Joseph A., S.J. *Paul and His Theology.* Englewood Cliffs, NJ: Prentice Hall, 1987.

Keck, Leander. *Paul and His Letters.* Philadelphia: Fortress, 1979.

Scroggs, Robin. *Paul for a New Day.* Philadelphia: Fortress, 1977.

Chapter 15. Justification

Achtemeier, Paul J. *Romans.* Atlanta: John Knox, 1985.

Fitzmyer, Joseph A., S.J. *Paul and His Theology.* Englewood Cliffs, NJ: Prentice Hall, 1987.

Kittel, Gerhard. "dikaiosune," *Theological Dictionary of the New Testament,* Vol. II. Grand Rapids: Eerdmans, 1964, 192–210.

Chapter 16. Paul's Many Images of Jesus

Fitzmyer, Joseph A., S.J. *Paul and His Theology.* Englewood Cliffs, NJ: Prentice Hall, 1987.

Richard, Earl. *Jesus: One and Many.* Wilmington: Glazier, 1988, 262–274, 295–332.

SUBJECT INDEX

OTHER BOOKS BY JOHN F. O'GRADY

Disciples and Leaders (Paulist Press, 1991)

The Four Gospels and the Jesus Tradition (Paulist Press, 1989)

The Story of the Apple Tree: A First Communion Book (Franciscan Communication, 1985)

Das Menschliche Antlitz Gottes (Walter, 1983)

The Gospel of John: Testimony of the Beloved Disciple (Pueblo, 1981)

Mark: The Sorrowful Gospel (Paulist Press, 1981)

Models of Jesus (Doubleday, 1981)

Individual and Community in John (Rome, 1978)

Christian Anthropology (Paulist Press, 1975)

Jesus, Lord and Christ (Paulist Press, 1973)

The Doctrine of Nature and Grace in the Writings of George Tyrrell (Rome, 1969)

DATE DUE

7/7/03			
MAY 0 3 2006			

Demco, Inc. 38-293